How Do I Pray?
The Bible Tells Us How

Written and illustrated by Jeff Todd

How Do I Pray? The Bible Tells Us How

© 2024 by Jeff Todd. All rights reserved.

Published by:
Jeff Todd
Newnan, Georgia

ISBN-13: 979-8-3304-9434-7

All rights reserved. No part of this publication may be reproduced or transmitted in any form or by any means without written permission of the author. All scriptural quotations are from the King James Version (KJV) of the Bible unless otherwise noted.

The purpose of this book is to share the Good News of Jesus Christ and put it out there in an easy-to-understand way. It is part of the outreach ministry of Jeff Todd.

Please note that there will be mistakes and misprints in this book. We are all human, right? We hope you won't find too many of them. This book was edited to the best of the author's ability and he will not be held responsible for errors.

Direct all correspondence to:

A BackPew Review
c/o Jeff Todd
PO Box 71972
Newnan, GA 30271-1972

Contents

Contents - 3

Introduction - 5

Why Do We Pray? And Why Is It So Important? - 11

How To Pray - 23

How Not To Pray - 55

When God Says No - 81

Answered Prayers (Why Did I Have To Wait So Long?) - 93

Remembering What We've Prayed - 105

Sinner's Prayer? What Is That? - 113

What Does It Mean To Be A Christian - 123

More From A BackPew Review - 175

The Introduction
By Lewis – The Common Tater

Reading the Bible freaks a lot of people out. Many feel that it's too complicated and should only be read by preachers or teachers and then translated so that they can understand it. Nope! That's the wrong way to look at it.

The fact is God's Word is for everybody. Anyone is able to make sense of it because God makes it possible through His Holy Spirit living within us. He will reveal spiritual things that apply to our life. For many of us, its just a matter of taking the time to open it up and read it.

If you knew that everything you needed to know about how to live life successfully was in there, wouldn't you want to read it for yourself? We also live in an age where people are listening to false doctrine and don't even know it. We don't take the time to compare what we are being told by preachers with what God's Word actually says. Many folks are being led astray. It's important to know the Truth! Try and think of the Bible as God's Words spoken directly to you on a personal level.

Since you have a copy of this book in your hand, you're probably wondering what it's all about. What's A BackPew Review? Right? If I had to give a quick answer, it's basically a simple man's perspective of what he receives from reading the Bible.

You see, I am an average ordinary person, just like you, that wants to live the Christian life the best way I can and hear what God is saying to me through His Word. I am basically writing down my thoughts from what I learn from the Bible and through life in general. I have no worldly qualifications, certifications or doctrinations that makes me the man for the job. I am a simple person – a nobody in the eyes of the world. However, I am saved and that makes me a child of God. And that's cool!

I also take the Great Commission seriously. Jesus told the disciples long ago to share the Gospel and take it to the four corners of the world. I feel that assignment was meant for us as well. Each one of us has a responsibility to let others know about Salvation – what it is and how to get it - and to tell someone what Jesus did for them on the cross.

For many of us, the questions are how do we do it and when can I get started? Right?

For me, I have to use what the Lord has given me. This includes the relationship I have with Jesus, His Word, and the gifts, talents, and characteristics that He molded into me from the day I was born. This also includes my ability to draw and write. Your gifts may be different, but are very important to God and should be used right away. And since Jesus is returning soon, the time you should begin sharing the Gospel is now.

I don't want you to get the wrong impression. The purpose of this book is not to be a substitute for reading the Bible. I feel everyone should read it. I don't want you to think I am poking fun at God's Word or trying to offend any religion. That's not my purpose. My hope and intentions for writing this book is that it will inspire you, as the reader, and will offer humorous illustrations to use in your walk with Christ. I want to present the Bible out there in a simple and easy-to-understand way so that everyone can get it. We can learn together how to live our life to its fullest with happiness and joy that God intended for us to live.

Hopefully, by reading this book, you'll see that being a Christian doesn't have to be boring and dull. I believe it should be energetic and alive like wired-up kids on a sugar high. We are to be a light in the world that we live in and shine out to others. When a person sees the way we are, it should make them want to be that way, too. Our lifestyle should point them to Jesus. Everything we say and do should reflect the One that saved us.

I have never considered myself to be like everyone else. The way I look at life may be different than the way others see it. Even as a young child, Christian people to me were always so serious and stiff-necked. It was almost like they were afraid to smile. I agree, it was wrong of me to segregate Christians like this, but those were the Christians I knew. As I grew older, I realized that some Christians were actually normal people and reflected Jesus in the way they acted.

I know from personal experience that being a Christian isn't hard. It's not a series of rituals or following a magic formula. It's actually so simple that anyone can be one. However, walking the Christian walk can be difficult and requires understanding of God's Word and applying it to our life. That's my purpose and focus of writing this book! I want to write something that would minister to people (no matter who they were) and possibly help them understand what it means to be a Christian and share with them the Gospel that leads them to eternal life.

It's got to be simple and easy to understand. I don't use BIG words when I speak, so I will not write BIG words when I am using this to reach people and lead them to Jesus. I can't! It's not how God made me! If you're reading this today, this book is for you from a simple-minded person like me. Being a Christian is awesome and it's not as weird as you may have heard. We're not crazy people! But, I am on a mission to show people how they can be saved.

One of the most important decisions we'll ever make is turning from our sinful nature and asking God for forgiveness. If you have never asked Jesus to come into your life, I hope and pray that you make that choice today.

Excuse me for a moment. I want to pray for you and for God's blessings on this book.

Dear Lord, I pray right now that You use these words from this book to reach people out there. Only You know who this is intended for and who will be reading this. I ask that you use it for Your glory and that this book will lead them to You. I give You all the praise and honor, Lord. Thank You for all that You do for me, Jesus. Amen.

This book is my personal commentary. I am sure there are several books floating out there and sermons preached around the world on the same thing, but this is what I received from doing my own personal study. It's a simple read.

If you find words that aren't spelled right, I'm sorry. If there are words left out, I apologize. This is about as good as it's going to get. I hope it is a blessing to you anyway and that you receive something from it.

So, here it is folks!

How Do I Pray?
The Bible Tells Us How

Why Do We Pray? And Why Is It So Important?

Why Do We Pray?
And Why Is It So Important?

I pray just like many of others out there in the world. I'm sure you pray, too. If you're a Christian (meaning that you are a follower of Jesus Christ), you started praying immediately after you surrendered your life to Him. It sorta just comes with the Christian-package. We've seen people do it and we just go with the flow. It's the thing to do. Right?

Early in our Christian life, praying is similar to the Aladdin story. You know the one. A young fella finds a dusty lamp and rubs it to get the dust off. All of a sudden a genie pops out and grants him three wishes. As a spiritually young Christian, we think of God as a genie that offers 'unlimited' wishes. We make those wishes by praying.

Yes, some 'prayer wishes' get answered and we get excited about it, but some don't. Or, they get answered in a way that we didn't expect. Or, we expect prayers to get answered right away and it seems like God (our Genie) is taking forever. This is when we get mad and give up on the whole 'praying thing' all together. Don't worry, we've all been there.

The dictionary says that prayer, in the Christian faith, is basically a solemn request for help or expression of thanks addressed to God. For many of us, that pretty much sums up what we do when we pray. We ask God for things and we thank Him for what He has already given us. We may pray every day or once a month or only on special occasions. We may pray long prayers that take several hours or only just a few seconds. Prayer is prayer. Is there really a guideline?

When we pray, we are recognizing God as the Creator of everything and that He is very able to give us our heart's desire if we should ask Him. We pray to Him because we know that He provides results. We may have seen Him answer the prayers of people that we know. So, we started doing it, too.

The Bible is full of stories where people have prayed to God. Someone may have had a burden that needed to be lifted, so they prayed. They must have known that God loved them enough to help them in their journey through life. They knew to reach out to Him in their time of need. Prayer was their way of communicating their need to God. God was their 'go to' for getting their needs and wants met. And praying was their way of getting it done. I'm sure God gets a lot of prayers and I have wondered if He ever gets tired of hearing them.

But, undoubtedly not. We are encouraged to pray. There are many scriptures that encourage us to pray. Here's a few:

Therefore I say unto you, What things soever ye desire, when ye pray, believe that ye receive them, and ye shall have them. - Mark 11: 24

And whatsoever ye shall ask in my name, that will I do, that the Father may be glorified in the Son. - John 14: 13

And all things, whatsoever ye shall ask in prayer, believing, ye shall receive. - Matthew 21: 22

When you read scriptures like these, you get the confidence in knowing that, when you pray to God, He hears you and will answer your prayers and give you what you ask Him for... as long as you believe. Right? I mean, that's what these scriptures say.

We all have needs and wants. Some of our spouses seem to have more than we do, but that's a different story. We also have times in our life where we face problems that we can't handle on our own. This is where being able to pray to God is wonderful. It's a great tool to have to make it through life. The Creator of everything we see is bigger than our problems. We're taking our 'big' problems to the Big Guy that created everything. I'm sure He doesn't have a problem in fixing them.

So, basically, praying is our way of getting the things we want? Kinda like the story of Aladdin? Yeah, but not exactly. It's more of the way we communicate with God. In our prayers, we can request Him to supply our needs. But, there is more that can be included in a prayer.

Prayers generally fall into five categories. From what I've read, here are the examples of the five types of prayer:

Blessing and Adoration Prayer

A prayer like this is one where we come to God and give Him praises by acknowledging to Him how great He is. It could begin like this, "Dear Lord, you are awesome! And here's why I feel this way..."

We all like to feel appreciated, especially when we have done something good for someone else. Am I right? Even the little things we do deserve some type of recognition. Here's an example:

I cut the grass around my home. My family expect it and they know that I am the only one out of our group that will do it. I don't see them going outside in the scorching heat in the middle of Summer to crank a mower. But, that's OK. I'm the one that does it and I do it for them... and to keep the HOA off my back. But, the point is that it needs to be done and I am the one that cuts the grass.

Do I get any recognition for it? Does my youngest daughter come up to me and say, "Dad, you're awesome for cutting grass so that I don't have to walk through a wilderness of weeds to catch the school bus!"? No!

Does my wife say, " Honey, I just want you to know that you're the best. I just love the way you cut our lawn and all that weed-eating that you do. You are just amazing. How about I cook you a special cake with sprinkles?"? Do I want this kind of recognition? Sometimes it would be nice to feel appreciated or recognized a little. It's not like it's going to hurt someone to say just a few good words every now and then.

I'm sure God feels this way, too. I bet He would like to hear His family say, "You're awesome for all that You do for us!" And He does more than cut weeds in our life. You know what I'm saying?

Thanksgiving prayer

This is a prayer where we thank God for what He has done in our life and for the things He has given us.

It's so easy to focus on the things that we don't have and we take for granted the things He has already given us. A prayer of 'thanks' would put our minds into focus, especially if we were to actually name the things we were thankful for in prayer.

My wife does a lot for our family. She cooks and tends to our kids. She does the shopping, which I would hate to do. Shopping requires time and strategic planning. I like to get my shopping done in five minutes. I don't want the stress. Sometimes she gets overwhelmed and a little stressed out over all the things she does. I can sympathize with this because I had to do it by myself for a few years when I was unemployed during the 2008 Economic Crisis. I know the feeling well. You feel unappreciated because these things we do for the family don't receive a paycheck, but they are equally important. A simple thing as saying 'thank you' goes a long way. By not saying 'thank you' sometimes will get you a frozen dinner that you zap in a microwave for two minutes. There's a big difference in the taste of a home-cooked meal cooked over a hot stove compared to a frozen dinner from a box. Let me tell you!

I'm sure God would like to hear how thankful we are for all that He has done for us. It would also do us some good by taking a moment to reflect on these things. We shouldn't take this stuff for granted.

Praise prayer

This is a prayer in which we give God glory for the many things and wonderful works He has done in our life.

Remember that thing you prayed for when it seemed impossible, but God did the impossible? Yeah, that one. This is where we would say thanks and give Him praises for His awesome way of getting it done.

To 'praise God' is basically expressing our feelings about Him and it seems to focus on His characteristics that we have learned through our own personal experiences. An example for me would be back a few years ago when my family and I were having financial trouble. I reached a point where I couldn't solve our money problems on my own and I had to reach out to God. I prayed and prayed about our situation and finally God reached down and answered my prayer. What did I learn? Well, for starters, God is powerful and can work miracles. No doubt! He is also my provider. Yes, He may choose to do it through my job. But, sometimes He likes to show out and provide for me without my help. So, from this, a simple prayer of praise from me would be, "Dear Lord, You are my Provider and You supply all of my needs. You are the reason I am able to make it day to day. Thank you for all that You do for me." Did you see how we can make a praise more personal to God? It was real because we experienced it.

Everybody has their own personal relationship with God and will learn more about Him as they grow spiritually. Whatever they learn through their life's experience with God will become part of their words of praise to Him.

Intercession (Supplication) Prayer

This is a prayer where we pray for our family and friends. We are coming before God and praying on their behalf.

Praying for others is a great thing to do and is encouraged from the scriptures:

I exhort therefore, that, first of all, supplications, prayers, intercessions, and giving of thanks, be made for all men; - 1 Timothy 2: 1

Many of our friends and family members have things going on in their life where they need someone to pray for them. We should lift them up to God. We should present their needs to God and request them on their behalf. If you think about it, if you have more than one person praying for the same thing for someone, it adds a little punch to the prayer request. I imagine it lets God know that we are serious about it and that we are willing to work as a team to present it to Him. I'm sure He gets excited when He sees a group working together towards one goal. It shows love for one another. He's all about love.

Petition prayer

This is a prayer where we ask God to fulfill a need in our life. This is the most common prayer that many of us do. It's fairly easy because we can always think of things that we need or want. All we have to do is present the request to God. Then, it's up to Him to decide if He wants to fill the order or not. Right?

For some, this the best part of being a Christian serving an Almighty God that wants to answer prayers. He's our Genie in a bottle that we whip out and rub when we want something. As funny and strange as this all sounds, it is how many of us treat God with our prayers. We have wants and God grants wishes. The Bible says to pray for it and He will give it to us. But, it sounds so one-sided. Surely there is more to it than this.

How To Pray

How To Pray

Do we really know how to pray? I'll admit. I have been praying the same way for several years. Sometimes I will have prayer thoughts inside my brain where I feel the need to talk to God. It's usually something quick and spontaneous. An example would be if I saw someone in distress, like a car wreck on the highway.

Inside my brain would be a quick prayer like "Dear Lord, help that family right there. I pray that everything will be OK for them. Amen."

Or, we'll be shopping and hear some kids acting crazy and terrorizing the store while their mother has that look of stressful desperation on her face.

"Dear Lord, be with that woman on Aisle 4. Give her patience and peace so that she doesn't hurt any of her children today and get arrested. Amen."

For the most part for me, my prayers are all done at night when I can finally get some peace and quiet. It's after the kids have went to bed, the phone has stopped ringing and no one is asking me for anything. During this time, I'll recap the day in my brain and think about my family, my home and our needs. I'll think about the things that God has done for us as a family unit and the things that He has already provided. I'll try and remember some of the posts that I have read on social media by people that are on my friend list and focus on the ones where people are going through hard times. I'll think on any wrong that I may have done that would go against God. All of this would become the elements of my prayer to Him for that night. Unfortunately, I get so side-tracked in my thoughts that I'll think about everything else that's not even related to prayer.

"Did I cut off the basement lights?"

"What tools will I need for the job I'm doing tomorrow?

"What would peanut butter taste like mixed with mayonnaise?"

These extra thoughts interrupt my prayer time. I'll bounce between 'thinking' and actually praying. I call it my ADHD Prayer and God knows all about it.

It's not that praying is difficult for me. It's not. It's finding that peaceful time to do it and to be able to get my thoughts together before I present them to God. It's also hard to stay focused on my communication with Him. Things were so much easier when I was a kid and all I had to do was remember the Children's Bedtime Prayer.

Do you remember this prayer we were taught as children?

The Children's Bedtime Prayer

For many us, we were taught at a young age on how to pray. We learned from watching others in church, at family gatherings where prayer is done before a big meal and we were taught to say the Children's Bedtime Prayer. If I remember correctly, it goes a little something like this:

*Now I lay me down to sleep
I pray the Lord my soul to keep
If I should die before I wake
I pray the Lord my soul to take*

*Bless Mommy and Daddy and...
(insert as many people as you want to pray for right here)
Amen.*

This was a nice poem prayer and it was easy to learn as a child. I find it funny that I can still remember it... and it's been roughly fifty years. All it's saying is basically 'Lord, keep me alive while I sleep. But, if die, take my soul to be with You. Also, bless my family and others...'. I don't see anything wrong with a prayer like this for a kid learning to pray. It gets them in a routine of praying to God every night before bedtime. It gives them an opportunity to think of others that may need someone to pray for them. I think that's awesome. However, praying this prayer when we get older may be a little weird. It can also become so repetitive that we lose any feelings in it. We're just saying a bunch of words with no heartfelt emotion.

Jesus Gave The Model Prayer

Learning how to pray can be taught by others, but I would personally go directly to the source. Jesus Christ would have the answer that we need and, believe it or not, has provided it in the scriptures. We call it The Lord's Prayer.

And it came to pass, that, as he was praying in a certain place, when he ceased, one of his disciples said unto him, Lord, teach us to pray, as John also taught his disciples. And he said unto them, When ye pray, say, Our Father which art in heaven, Hallowed be thy name. Thy kingdom come. Thy will be done, as in heaven, so in earth. Give us day by day our daily bread. And forgive us our sins; for we also forgive every one that is indebted to us. And lead us not into temptation; but deliver us from evil. - Luke 11: 1-4

Jesus was praying alone when one of His disciples walked up and sees Him doing it. I assume the disciple thought it was kinda cool and wanted Jesus to teach him how he could do it, too. And Jesus didn't hold back. He gave him a prayer example. This prayer consists of key elements that we should include in our prayer to God. These are called seven petitions.

1. Our Father, Which Art In Heaven (Not A Petition, But More Of Whom We Should Be Addressing)

God is our Heavenly Father. Just like our Dads on Planet Earth, God loves and cares for His children. Our relationship with Him should be similar to the one we have with our Dads. There is so much to say here, so I included more details about it in the upcoming paragraphs.

2. Hallowed Be Thy Name

Hallowed means holy or sanctified. God's name is holy.

There is none holy as the Lord: for there is none beside thee: neither is there any rock like our God. - 1 Samuel 2: 2

As Christians, we understand that God is to be revered and praised above all else. In this petition, we pray that the entire world will recognize the holy name of God as the one true God of all - the Creator and Ruler of the universe.

2. Thy Kingdom Come

This petition has two purposes. One, we pray for the Kingdom of God to take form in the here and now so that we can live in a world that is characterized by faith, hope and love.

And now abideth faith, hope, charity, these three; but the greatest of these is charity. - 1 Corinthians 13: 13

Two, we pray that the promise of a 'new heaven and a new earth' be fulfilled. When that promise is fulfilled, the faithful will live with God in His Kingdom eternally as members of a Holy City in which there is no death, crying or pain.

And I saw a new heaven and a new earth: for the first heaven and the first earth were passed away; and there was no more sea. And I John saw the holy city, new Jerusalem, coming down from God out of heaven, prepared as a bride adorned for her husband. And I heard a great voice out of heaven saying, Behold, the tabernacle of God is with men, and he will dwell with them, and they shall be his people, and God himself shall be with them, and be their God. And God shall wipe away all tears from their eyes; and there shall be no more death, neither sorrow, nor crying, neither shall there be any more pain: for the former things are passed away. -
Revelation 21: 1-4

3. Thy Will Be Done, As In Heaven, So In Earth.

God reigns from Heaven with compassion and justice. His will is that we praise Him and love one another. We know this because Jesus tells us in the Bible.

Jesus said unto him, Thou shalt love the Lord thy God with all thy heart, and

with all thy soul, and with all thy mind. This is the first and great commandment. And the second is like unto it, Thou shalt love thy neighbour as thyself. On these two commandments hang all the law and the prophets. - Matthew 22: 37-40

Praying this petition is an act of surrender to the will of God. By doing so, we request here for God to give us the strength to follow His will - not ours - in living a life that gives Him glory and shows compassion to others.

4. Give Us Day By Day Our Daily Bread

Food nourishes the body. God's Word nourishes the soul. The Bible tells us that that we can't live on bread alone, but by every word that comes from the mouth of the Lord.

And he humbled thee, and suffered thee to hunger, and fed thee with manna, which thou knewest not, neither did thy fathers know; that he might make thee know that man doth not live by bread only, but by every word that proceedeth out of the mouth of the Lord doth man live. - Deuteronomy 8: 3

In this petition, we pray for spiritual food so that we can have the courage to go out into the world and spread His Message through our words and actions. This nourishment comes from the Word of God and from our relationship with Jesus. Jesus is our bread of life.

I am that bread of life. - John 6: 48

I am the living bread which came down from heaven: if any man eat of this bread, he shall live for ever: and the bread that I will give is my flesh, which I will give for the life of the world. - John 6: 51

5. And Forgive Us Our Sins; For We Also Forgive Every One That Is Indebted To Us

This petition may be hard for many of us to pray. It's easy to ask for forgiveness from God, but can we truly forgive others of the wrong that they have done to us? Keep this thought in mind. Being able to forgive them can totally transform your life.

Sometimes forgiving someone is hard to do in person. But according to scripture, forgiving them in prayer to God may make things easier.

And when ye stand praying, forgive, if ye have ought against any: that your Father also which is in heaven may forgive you your trespasses. - Mark 11: 25

By choosing to replace resentment with forgiveness, we show God's love and mercy in our actions. This, in turn, helps us to walk toward God with confidence. He wants us to walk our path of life towards Him.

6. And Lead Us Not Into Temptation

Temptation can lead us to sin and away from God. God doesn't lead us to sin, but because we have free will and we are born with a sinful nature, it's easy for us to become a victim of sin. Thankfully, God is faithful and promises to provide a way out of any temptation that we may face.

There hath no temptation taken you but such as is common to man: but God is faithful, who will not suffer you to be tempted above that ye are able; but will with the temptation also make a way to escape, that ye may be able to bear it. - 1 Corinthians 10: 13

In this petition, we are accepting the fact that our free will brings with it human weaknesses. To overcome those weaknesses, we pray for God to guide us away from temptation and give us the discernment to know when we are confronted with it and to steer us away.

7. But Deliver Us From Evil
Because we are weak when it comes to spiritual matters. This petition is a request to God to deliver us from temptation and sin and all that evil brings. The scriptures tell us that He will.

I sought the Lord, and he heard me, and delivered me from all my fears. - Psalm 34: 4

It's basically a request of protection. The world has so much to offer us that we can easily get entangled in sin. And sin leads to death.

What Does It All Mean?
The Lord's Prayer is much more than a guide on what to pray when you can't think of anything to say. The prayer, if we think on each petition, serves as a moral compass that reveals the best way to go before God in requesting His guidance and protection.

The Lord's Prayer focuses our thoughts on what's important in life by summarizing all that we must do to be 'good and faithful servants'. Basically to give God reverence, accept His will, know His Word, love each other through forgiveness and to resist evil.

Pray According To His Will
Before I formed thee in the belly I knew thee; - Jeremiah 1: 5a

The scriptures tell us that God knew us while we were being created in our mother's belly. Even though the scripture above was directed toward Jeremiah, it also lets me know that He knew that we would be born, too. I believe babies are gifts from Him. I also believe that He has a purpose for the ones that He has allowed to be born. If we are living and breathing today, God has a purpose for us.

For I know the thoughts that I think toward you, saith the Lord, thoughts of peace, and not of evil, to give you an expected end. Then shall ye call upon me, and ye shall go and pray unto me, and I will hearken unto you. And ye shall seek me, and find me, when ye shall search for me with all your heart. - Jeremiah 29: 11-13

He also has a will for our lives. There are things that He wants us to do. There are things that He wants us to have to fulfill the purpose that He has for us.

And this is the confidence that we have in him, that, if we ask any thing according to his will, he heareth us: And if we know that he hear us, whatsoever we ask, we know that we have the petitions that we desired of him. - 1 John 5: 14, 15

Since we know that the reason we are here is to serve God, then our prayers should align with the things that He would want for us. The things we should ask of Him should be the things that would help us serve Him better or fill a need in our life that would, in turn, continue our service to Him.

I have heard of preachers that teach their listeners to basically pray for anything. They would say, "Name it and claim it!" As if God would give a person anything their heart desired.

"Lord, I want a brand new pink Mercedes Benz with purple fluffy dice on the rear view mirror! Amen."

"Dear God, I want a mansion! Nothing special, as long as it has 30 bedrooms, 10 bathrooms and a huge kitchen for my family of five. Oh! Could you hurry up with this request? My rent is due! Amen."

"Oh, Jesus! I need a wife. The other ones I had weren't any good. I want this one I found on page 32 of this swanky magazine. She doesn't look like she could cook, but I'm willing to make sacrifices. Thank you, Jesus. Amen."

God doesn't work that way. It's not that He couldn't answer the prayer just the way we wanted. He has a will for our lives and some things just don't fit His plans for us.

Pray Without Ceasing

Rejoice evermore. Pray without ceasing. In every thing give thanks: for this is the will of God in Christ Jesus concerning you. - 1 Thessalonians 5: 16-18

Praying without ceasing? To pray without stopping for air? To try and think of the words to say for a whole day of prayer? I'm not sure that I have what it takes to make this happen. I just don't like to talk that much. Surely this doesn't mean what I think it means. Does it?

Prayer is how we communicate with God. I mean, you can't see Him in person. To be honest, we couldn't handle His holy presence anyway because we would all die from shock. But, through prayer we can talk to Him and present our request and concerns.

If you're having a bad day, tell God about it. If you're stressed, talk to Him. If you find yourself all alone with no one to talk to, well... there you go. Talk to God.

But, who wants to talk all day... other than my four year old granddaughter? Praying without ceasing? What could this mean?

Continue in prayer, and watch in the same with thanksgiving. - Colossians 4: 2

I think it simply has to do with keeping God in our thoughts throughout the day. When there's a quiet moment, use it to mentally speak to God. Give Him thanks for everything that He has done for you. Just talk to him about anything. Do it inside your mind and try not move your lips while in public. That could create a scene that could lead you into a padded room wearing a straight jacket. Just keep it to yourself. Know what I mean?

Be Bold In Prayer

Let us therefore come boldly unto the throne of grace, that we may obtain mercy, and find grace to help in time of need. - Hebrews 4: 16

The quick definition of 'being bold' is simply having confidence and being courageous. That's it. The opposite of this would be to have fear. When it comes to prayer time, what is our emotional feeling when we bring our request to God? Do we dread asking Him for anything? Or can we boldly tell Him what we need? According to this scripture, God is willing to help us in our times of need. I guess the real question is how do we view God?

I know there are people out there that were taught to fear Him. They felt that if they did something wrong in life, He would strike them down with a lightning bolt from Heaven. They lived their Christian life in fear. But, as we read the Bible, we learn that God is love.

Beloved, let us love one another: for love is of God; and every one that loveth is born of God, and knoweth God. He that loveth not knoweth not God; for God is love. - 1 John 4: 7, 8

God loves us and wants what is best for His people. Just as we would boldly go to someone (a parent or friend) that we know that loves us and ask for anything, we should do the same to God in prayer. There's no need for fear – be bold.

Pray In Private

But thou, when thou prayest, enter into thy closet, and when thou hast shut thy door, pray to thy Father which is in secret; and thy Father which seeth in secret shall reward thee openly. - Matthew 6: 6

Prayer is a special moment between you and God. You are communicating with the Creator of the world. He's the one that took the time to create you. He's your Maker. Prayer is when you set aside time to talk to Him and let Him know what is on your mind. This will include giving Him your thanks for what He has done for you. This is when you can tell Him about the things you need. Nobody else needs to hear your conversation. It's special and private. Don't treat it like posting a status update on social media. I say again, no one needs to know your business.

There are people that love praying when there is a crowd around them. It gives them a moment to impress them with their fancy words and dramatic actions. The people that see this are amazed at how elegant this person is and how they are able to pray with such finesse. If only they themselves could pray so good. Right? Unfortunately, God isn't about the show. He would rather have a one-on-one relationship with the individual in private.

I've been a Christian long enough to have seen people that like to show off their prayer techniques. I will admit, it is impressive. The emotional tears, the falling to the floor in dramatics and those elegant words... a normal person would need to carry around a pocket dictionary to know what some of those fancy words mean. But, these same people get chosen every time to pray at special events and occasions.

Pray About Everything
Be careful for nothing; but in every thing by prayer and supplication with thanksgiving let your requests be made known unto God. And the peace of God, which passeth all understanding, shall keep your hearts and minds through Christ Jesus. - Philippians 4: 6-7

"I found us a great deal on an XYZ vacation trip in a few months if we go ahead and make our reservations now...", my wife says at least four times a year.

"Do we have the money to do it?" which is my usual reply.

"Of course. All the bills are paid this month." she replies each and every time.

"Well, you handle writing those checks for the bills around here. You see our bank balances every month. If you think we can do it, I guess it's OK." I say usually with dread and nervousness.

She will make the reservation and she plans the vacation. But, during the waiting period, we will get what I call 'surprise bills' that we wished we had used that money on. So, we scramble to find the funds to get them paid. We end up working extra hard for the next few months. Maybe we should have prayed about it instead. Now we're tired from working so hard to get a vacation to the point that we are now tired when we should be relaxing.

Praying about everything creates peace. And peace brings joy and happiness. A simple thing as making vacation plans, God can make it work so much easier with no stress. This would apply to anything in life. Pray about it first. Now, how should I go about relaying this message to my wife?

Pray For Your Enemies

But I say unto you which hear, Love your enemies, do good to them which hate you, Bless them that curse you, and pray for them which despitefully use you. - Luke 6: 27-28

I don't have enemies. This is probably because I don't do social circles. I don't go out of my way to socialize with people. I'm not a member of any clubs, groups or organizations. I have only a handful of friends. Even on my job, I work with family, so there's no stepping on people to get higher on the corporate ladder. Nobody really gets mad at one another, unless somebody accidentally drops a sheet of plywood on the other one's toe or forgets to tell everyone that they freshly painted some trim that is now smeared on our hands. But, after calling each other a few names that I can't say here, we all get over it and move on.

Every now and then I will have a booth at one of them comic conventions. The only purpose is to share these books with people. My friend that hangs out with me at these shows laughs at me because I purposely don't interact with people. He does all the talking about the books and illustrations. I classify myself as 'anti-social', and when you're anti-social, you shouldn't have to worry about having enemies. I mean, you barely have friends. Right?

In the 'real' world there are people that don't like you. They want your job title, your lifestyle and anything you got that they don't have. Because you have to face them everyday, you feel their hate and jealousy. These are the people that you have to pray for. Even though they don't like you, you have to love them and do good towards them. It doesn't seem fair, does it?

God has a higher standard for His people and wants us to be more like Jesus. It helps us to become more compassionate towards others.

"Dear Lord, I want to pray for Steve. He is such a jerk at work. He gives me such a hard time. I think he wants me to quit my job. Something just isn't right about him. Help him, Lord, with whatever is going on in his life. Amen."

Steve may have issues at home or has been battling something he has had going on since he was a child. By being compassionate towards him and praying for him, God can work on that side of the coin and help him. The alternative would be to meet him after work in the parking lot and settle things yourself. Violence never solves anything and usually makes matters worse.

Forgive Others Before Praying

And when ye stand praying, forgive, if ye have ought against any: that your Father also which is in heaven may forgive you your trespasses. - Mark 11: 25

This scripture can be a hard pill to swallow for some of us. For starters, the scriptures say that God doesn't hear our prayers when we have sin in our lives. Secondly, God will not forgive our sins if we don't forgive the people that have sinned against us. So, if we don't take care of these issues, saying a prayer would be like blowing air into the wind. This could be why we feel that God doesn't answer our prayers. We got some work to do.

Are we holding grudges against people? Is there someone that we have completely wiped out of our life because we simply don't want to deal with the issue? Well, we got to forgive them. We could probably do it in person or we could simply forgive them in prayer to God. We have to release it or we will suffer.

I read on the Internet about the consequences of bitterness (lack of forgiveness) and how it affects the body - physically, mentally, emotionally, and spiritually. It's real interesting. Here's what I found:

Physical Consequences
- *Chemical Imbalance*
  Resentment causes an imbalance in the hormones from the various glands of the body, producing many physical symptoms and diseases.
- *Weakened Immune System*
  The stress of bitterness weakens the immune system and make you prone to physical ailments. Often doctors can trace physical disorders to a point in time when bitterness began to develop.
- *The Appearance of Premature Aging*
  Refusal to forgive causes fatigue and loss of sleep. Soon your eyes and facial features reflect your inner distress. Before long, you're looking like an old lady... and you're only 23!

Mental and Emotional Consequences
- *Depression*
  It takes emotional energy to maintain a grudge. When your emotional energy is exhausted, you become depressed.
- *Stress*
  Hating someone produces stress hormones in your body. You become worn out and unable to cope with daily challenges.
- *Destructive Emotional Focus*

Bitterness and resentment create an emotional focus toward the person who offended you. This focus causes you to become like the one you resent. The more you think about his actions, the more you begin to reflect the basic attitudes that prompted his actions.

Spiritual Consequences

- *Unable To Love God*
  "If a man say, I love God, and hateth his brother, he is a liar: for he that loveth not his brother whom he hath seen, how can he love God whom he hath not seen? And this commandment have we from him, that he who loveth God love his brother also." - I John 4: 20–21
- *Doubts About Our Relationship With God*
  Jesus said, *"For if ye forgive men their trespasses, your heavenly Father will also forgive you: but if ye forgive not men their trespasses, neither will your Father forgive your trespasses." - Matthew 6: 14–15*
- *Major Stumbling Blocks In The Spiritual Development Of Others*
  Bitterness is easily passed from one generation to another, and it will have a significant impact on your children.

Thou shalt not bow down thyself unto them, nor serve them: for I the Lord thy God am a jealous God, visiting the iniquity of the fathers upon the children unto the third and fourth generation of them that hate me - Deuteronomy 5: 9

Attitudes of bitterness also cause your family, friends, and acquaintances to discredit your Christian testimony.

I think it would be easier to just go on ahead and forgive those people. There's so much to lose by not doing so. You agree?

Pray For The Sick
Is any sick among you? let him call for the elders of the church; and let them pray over him, anointing him with oil in the name of the Lord: And the prayer of faith shall save the sick, and the Lord shall raise him up; and if he have committed sins, they shall be forgiven him. - James 5: 14-15

People get sick. That's just how it goes in life. Sick people need folks praying for them. The scriptures tell us that we should include them in our prayers. Take a look around your circle of friends and family. Anybody sick? They need prayer and the person doing it should be you. Lift them up in prayer. Does this mean that we should pray for their complete healing?

When I was young (maybe around 14), I went to bed one night with a sore throat. It really wasn't anything life crippling. It didn't hurt. It was just uncomfortable and annoying. I prayed to God that night and asked Him to heal my throat. I kept repeating the prayer and amazingly I felt the annoying feeling in my throat go away. I believe God healed my throat that day. It scared the stew out of me. The memory has stayed with me all of these years. So, I know God is able to heal.

On a different example a few years ago, my Mom called me in tears on the phone. She told me that her head was hurting real bad. My spiritual connection with God was in check and I felt the need to pray for her on the phone for a complete healing of her pain. I was sincere and I believed that God was able to perform the miracle I was about to request. My faith in Him was in check.

I told her to hold on while I prayed and that God was about to do a miracle in her life. I knelt on the ground outside as I kept the cordless phone to my ear. I sincerely told God about the problem and asked for His help. After I prayed, I asked her how she felt. I was expecting her to tell me that the pain in her head was gone and that a miracle just happened. But, no. The pain was still there. This cut me to the core. What happened? Did I not have enough faith? Did she not have enough faith for this to happen?

What went wrong? God didn't heal her and I was left speechless. Why didn't this work?

My Mom called me a few days later to tell me that she had went to the doctor. He had given her some kind of medicine and now her head was feeling so much better. Did God put a delay on her healing? Or did a doctor make it happen instead? This made me question how God healed people.

He healed me before and there are countless of stories of how God has healed people. So, what is the 'trick' on getting God to heal the sick people we are praying for?

There are many religious shows on TV and 'public shows' where so-called evangelical preachers bop you on the head or 'speak the power of healing' on someone and miraculously they are healed of whatever ailed them. I'm sorry, but I can't believe any of it. It's not that I don't believe God could do it. He can! But, a miracle like this would have to bring God glory and not the person making a spectacle of it.

I know that in the New Testament, the disciples were given the gift of healing people. It was the power of God working though them to make the miracle happen. It would happen when a crowd formed. I believe the purpose was to show unbelievers that God was real because immediately they became believers. It wasn't a 'show', it was more of a tool to reach people that didn't know who Jesus was.

So, what are we really doing when we pray for the sick? Our prayers should center around God's will. What would be His will for the sick person that we are praying for? We don't know. But, we are trusting that He knows the best way to handle it.

It could be that He wants to heal them completely. Or, He will give them the strength to endure what they are going through. It could be that He wants the people around the sick person to seek Him or see His glory through this situation.

It could be that the sick person doesn't know God and through this predicament, he reaches out to Him. He will forgive his sins and raise him up – meaning to take him home to be with Him.

Pray To God - Your Father
But to us there is but one God, the Father, of whom are all things, and we in him; and one Lord Jesus Christ, by whom are all things, and we by him. - 1 Corinthians 8: 6

A father of the fatherless, and a judge of the widows, is God in his holy habitation. - Psalm 68: 5

And will be a Father unto you, and ye shall be my sons and daughters, saith the Lord Almighty. - 2 Corinthians 6: 18

When Jesus gave the example of prayer (The Lord's Prayer) from the scriptures, He prayed to God... our Father. God is our Father? Does that sound normal to you? For some of you, that's pretty cool. You have your experiences with your earthly Dad and you also have a Heavenly one. Sounds awesome, doesn't it? Two Dads... how sweet. You are blessed to have an earthly Dad. Any time, while on Earth and have a need, all you have to do is call your Dad and he will be there for you.

But, what about people that never had the opportunity to have a Dad here on Earth? They don't know this whole 'Dad Experience'. They don't know what this would be like. Who would they call? Hopefully, for them, they had their Mom to love and nurture them. But some didn't. So, how is a person going to know how to see God as their Father? They've never experienced it before.

According to my research, there is a father absence in America. There are 19.7 million kids out there that will never experience having a father in their life. That's more than 1 kid out of 4. This study probably doesn't include the adults that continue with life without this experience. This figure just blows my mind. Yes, some of these kids will do OK in life without their father. But, will they know how to relate to God to their fullest as their Father spiritually? Probably not.

Look. This hits home with me. I have only seen my biological father a few times in my lifetime. Was he a bad person? No. He was a good person the few times that I met him. He just didn't want to be a parent. Do I hate him? No. The more I focus on God, I have developed compassion towards a man that is lost that will one day realize what he has forsaken. He has missed out on years of seeing me grow to become a man. He is missing out on his grandchildren and their children. He has become a lonely man missing out on the blessings of God. It's a sad story.

How does this affect me? Well, I don't really know how to accept God as my Father. I know I should, but I don't really know what that should feel like. I am OK with seeing God as my friend. I mean, I have friends... not many... but, they are true friends that reach out to me when I have needs. I know what this experience is like. In return, I am a good friend. I will gladly help people that I care about. Just say the word and I am there. No questions asked.

I'm even cool with seeing God as a 'boss'. No big deal. If God needs me to do anything for His glory or for any type of Kingdom work, I am there. I'll do whatever He wants me to do. If He wants me to do a mission trip, I'll be the first one on the plane. If God wants me to write books to share His Word and to tell the world about Jesus, I don't have a problem with that. I'll keep going until He tells me to stop. No problem.

But, for me to call Him 'Father'?... umm, I'm not too sure how to do that. How do you feel about it?

The point is... God is our Father in Heaven. The scriptures tell us that He will even be a father to the fatherless. There's no escaping that truth from His Word. It's sad that the world is in this parental crisis. But, I would bet that Satan has a hand in all of this mess. If he can keep the children away from knowing God as a Father in their life, he will have accomplished a major task – by us not knowing God on a personal level.

Hopefully for us, we have broken the chains of what life without a father has done to us. I would hope that we can be the father to our children that we didn't have. We can then take what we have learned about what being a father should be and see what God is and should be to us. According to the scriptures, He is our Father that just so happens to live in Heaven. That's pretty awesome right there!

How Not To Pray

How Not To Pray

Don't Pray Like A Hypocrite

For what is the hope of the hypocrite, though he hath gained, when God taketh away his soul? Will God hear his cry when trouble cometh upon him? - Job 27: 8-9

And when thou prayest, thou shalt not be as the hypocrites are: for they love to pray standing in the synagogues and in the corners of the streets, that they may be seen of men. Verily I say unto you, They have their reward. But thou, when thou prayest, enter into thy closet, and when thou hast shut thy door, pray to thy Father which is in secret; and thy Father which seeth in secret shall reward thee openly. But when ye pray, use not vain repetitions, as the heathen do: for they think that they shall be heard for their much speaking. Be not ye therefore like unto them: for your Father knoweth what things ye have need of, before ye ask him. - Matthew 6: 5-8

A dictionary tells me that a hypocrite is a person who pretends to have virtues (moral or religious beliefs, principles, etc.) that he or she does not actually possess. They're fake... a phony... they're not the real deal!

Praying like a hypocrite would basically be someone that may appear to be all holy and so in tune with God in their prayers. But, the truth is that they are fake and their words don't mean Jack Squat! For those of you unfamiliar with Southern slang, the term "Jack Squat' means 'nothing, zero, zilch,...zip'. Feel free to use it.

These people simply want to be seen and heard by others. They perform their 'religious show' in front of groups of people. If we didn't know any better, we would assume that someone like this would be the example of how we should model our prayer life. God knows our hearts and can see right through it. He's not about fake people.

You will find this in churches today, especially when a group asks someone to lead in prayer. I'm sure this person feels the pressure of his peers. Their eyes and ears are upon him and this person wants to make sure that his words sound pleasant to the audience. His focus may not be entirely on God, but more to the people that are bowing their heads and listening to him. It's interesting to hear because this same person that came to church that day, who normally speaks Southern English with slang words, is now speaking the same Old English written in the Bible. Thee... thou... thee... thine... you get the idea. Their prayer sounds more like a Shakespeare play. To me, this is phony. Why not pray like a normal person? Pray in Southern English!

Beware of the scribes, which desire to walk in long robes, and love greetings in the markets, and the highest seats in the synagogues, and the chief rooms at feasts; Which devour widows' houses, and for a show make long prayers: the same shall receive greater damnation - Luke 20: 46-47

A scribe back in the day was a person whose main job was to copy royal and sacred manuscripts. They were the 'photocopying machine' of the ancient times. They enjoyed being seen wearing their long robes, being in the presence of large crowds, sitting with the people in high authority and praying long-winded prayers that was more for show. These were fake people, too. God didn't care too much for these kinds of people either.

People in churches today are guilty. They may not wear the long robes, but they sure look good in a three-piece suit. Their accessories of jewelry and overpowering cologne has given many church members the feeling that these people are so close to God in their walk that they should appoint them as leaders of their church. They should also be the ones to call if they need someone to lead them in prayer because they pray so long with such finesse.

But, according to the Bible, that's not how we should pray. God wants His people to be sincere when it comes to prayer. He wants us to talk to Him privately and not do it for an audience. Prayer is meant to be a one-on-one experience with our Creator – not a Broadway performance. Get me?

Don't Pray With Sin In Your Life

There are a lot of scriptures in the Bible about how God doesn't hear the prayers of people with sin in their lives.

The Lord is far from the wicked: but he heareth the prayer of the righteous. - Proverbs 15: 29

And when ye spread forth your hands, I will hide mine eyes from you: yea, when ye make many prayers, I will not hear: your hands are full of blood. - Isaiah 1: 15

He that turneth away his ear from hearing the law, even his prayer shall be abomination. - Proverbs 28: 9

Yea, they made their hearts as an adamant stone, lest they should hear the law, and the words which the Lord of hosts hath sent in his spirit by the former prophets: therefore came a great wrath from the Lord of hosts. Therefore it is come to pass, that as he cried, and they would not hear; so they cried, and I would not hear, saith the Lord of hosts. - Zechariah 7: 12-13

If I regard iniquity in my heart, the Lord will not hear me. - Psalm 66:18

But your iniquities have separated between you and your God, and your sins have hid his face from you, that he will not hear. - Isaiah 59: 2

For the eyes of the Lord are over the righteous, and his ears are open unto their prayers: but the face of the Lord is against them that do evil. - 1 Peter 3: 12

Then shall they call upon me, but I will not answer; they shall seek me early, but they shall not find me: For that they hated knowledge, and did not choose the fear of the Lord: They would none of my counsel: they despised all my reproof. - Proverbs 1: 28-30

That's a lot of scripture. It should show the importance of knowing that God is holy and how our sin separates us from Him. As long as we are living with sin in our life, God will not hear us when we pray to Him. This could be the reason that some people feel like their prayers are going unanswered. It could be why sometimes we feel that our prayers don't go any further than the ceiling.

If you know that you are doing something wrong in your life that goes against God's will for you, the first thing you should do is ask Him for forgiveness of it and turn away from this sinful lifestyle. If you don't, your prayers will be hindered. Jesus asked for forgiveness in His prayer model that He gave His disciples. He knew that we would all sin, so our prayer to God should include a sincere request for forgiveness. By doing so, it would open the prayers lines and provide clarity for the rest of what we are praying.

An example of a sincere prayer starter would be, *"Dear Lord, forgive me of all of my sins..."* From there, we can continue with confidence that God is listening.

Don't Pray Like A Self-Centered Person

Ye ask, and receive not, because ye ask amiss, that ye may consume it upon your lusts. - James 4: 3

The word 'lust' is more than just wanting to fulfill sexual desires according to the Bible. Lust is defined as a strong desire for someone or something. It caters to our sinful nature of wanting everything to be all about us. There are a lot of things that people could lust for such as money, power, food, drink, fame and knowledge. It's really about wanting the things that will make us happy. If we pray for those things, God sees our hearts and may choose not to answer those prayers.

Examples of praying for money:

"Dear Lord, I want to be rich. I want a big house, twenty cars and a bank account full of money. If you give me these things, I will never have to worry again. I might even donate a portion to a charity of Your choice. Amen."

"Dear Lord, thank you for all that You have given me. I am grateful. My wife and I just received a surprise bill in the mail today and we don't have the funds to pay it. If we don't pay, we're going to lose the thing we're paying for. Please, if it's Your will, provide us with the money to pay our debt. Thank you. Amen."

Which of these prayers sounds more like a prayer that is aligned with God?

Famous preachers on TV will tell you, that if you give money to their church, God will give you a blessing of money that is way more than what you gave. Their proposal sounds more like a money-making investment as if God is selling stocks into His Kingdom that guarantees large financial gain from each investment – regardless of how small it is. They will say, "God loves a cheerful giver.", which is taken out of context from 2 Corinthians 9: 7. But, people happily give with the hopes that they will receive a healthy return. Even though they 'give', the reason is more of a self-centered motive. That's why I feel this is wrong. I don't believe God works this way.

I remember a TV pastor walking on stage with a shovel several years ago. On the right side of him was a pile of money. He scooped up some money with his shovel and told his viewers that, if they gave this much money, God would bless them with more. He showed this by scooping several loads of money with his shovel and filling up a wheelbarrow. Even as a kid watching this, I knew this was wrong. It just didn't seem right. This pastor was trying to manipulate people by using their lust of wanting more money for themselves. I mean, the claim sounds great. Can you imagine God as an investment program? Who would need a savings account, stocks or bonds.... or even a 401K plan? Invest in God and His church with the weird looking preacher.... that's a guaranteed return on our investment. Right? Wrong!

Examples of praying for power and fame:

"Dear Lord, a new job has been created at work. Well, I want that job. It's a leader position and I think I deserve it. It pays so much more than I get now. It will raise my position in life to a higher level. I can begin socializing with the upper class. I can start going to the fancier places for dining, travel and see the world and I could even upgrade my old pickup truck for something a little more eye-catching. My name would have meaning and people would have to listen to me for a change. I need this job, Lord. Make it happen, Cap'n. Amen."

"Dear Lord, thank you for blessing me with a large family. I'm not complaining, but we're starting to run out of room. As you already know, our latest addition sleeps with us at night because we don't have the space or funds to build a room addition to our house. However, there is a job that just got posted at work. It pays more and I feel that I am qualified for it. It's a leader position, and because of what You have taught me as the leader of my family and the fact that I have been with this company for ten years, I think that I would be a valuable asset to them. In turn, I could use the income to improve our situation at home. Lord, if it's Your will, I would like to have this job. Amen."

Which of these prayers sounds more like a prayer that is aligned with God?

It's all about the purpose behind our prayers. God may choose not to answer the ones that have self-centered motives. What would God want us to have?

Don't Pray Like A Terrible Husband

Likewise, ye husbands, dwell with them according to knowledge, giving honour unto the wife, as unto the weaker vessel, and as being heirs together of the grace of life; that your prayers be not hindered. - 1 Peter 3: 7

I stumbled across this scripture and found it interesting. It talks about husbands and how their prayers can be hindered based on how they treat their wives. From what it says, if you're a husband that treats your wife like crap, the answers to your prayers can be affected. It could be in the form of delays or worse, God may not answer them at all. This is serious.

We probably need to evaluate how we are treating our wives. It plainly says that we are to be working together as a married couple. We are a team. According to the vows we made, we were joined together in the presence of God. We became one.

For this cause shall a man leave his father and mother, and shall be joined unto his wife, and they two shall be one flesh. - Ephesians 5: 31

The only solution is to make things right. We got to start honoring our wives. Treat them with respect – as partners in marriage. If your wife is whining and complaining about your relationship, maybe you should listen. Come up with ways to improve it instead of pushing her aside and labeling her as a nag. Your response will affect the outcome of your prayers.

Other Examples Of "Don't Pray Like..."

People That Offer Unworthy Service To God
Ye offer polluted bread upon mine altar; and ye say, Wherein have we polluted thee? In that ye say, The table of the Lord is contemptible. And if ye offer the blind for sacrifice, is it not evil? and if ye offer the lame and sick, is it not evil? offer it now unto thy governor; will he be pleased with thee, or accept thy person? saith the Lord of hosts. And now, I pray you, beseech God that he will be gracious unto us: this hath been by your means: will he regard your persons? saith the Lord of hosts. - Malachi 1: 7-9

People knew what God expected from them in their sacrifices to Him, but they chose to offer something else. It was definitely not their best. According to these verses, instead of their best animal from their herd, they would offer Him a blind one that was sick or had something wrong with it. It was almost like they gave God what they had left from the bottom of the barrel. Maybe they knew their best would benefit them better for their own personal gain, so they offered God something useless with very little value. God wasn't pleased with this and it affected their prayers.

I know that we don't use animals as sacrifices to God anymore. But, we can still offer Him sacrifices that don't eat hay and stink up a barnyard. Here are those sacrifices that please God:

1. We sacrifice with our lips
   By him therefore let us offer the sacrifice of praise to God continually, that is, the fruit of our lips giving thanks to his name. But to do good and to communicate forget not: for with such sacrifices God is well pleased. - Hebrews 13: 15-16

God wants to hear our praises and our words of thankfulness for all that He has done for us. Who wouldn't? We have a lot to thank Him for and we should tell Him. We should include this in our prayers.

2. We sacrifice with our life
   I beseech you therefore, brethren, by the mercies of God, that ye present your bodies a living sacrifice, holy, acceptable unto God, which is your reasonable service. And be not conformed to this world: but be ye transformed by the renewing of your mind, that ye may prove what is that good, and acceptable, and perfect, will of God. - Romans 12: 1-2

   Live your life for God. Do the things that He has asked us to do from His Word. If you're a Christian, act like one. If it means changing your surroundings of friends and people, do it. Be who God wants you to be.

3. We sacrifice with our possessions
   Or he that exhorteth, on exhortation: he that giveth, let him do it with simplicity; he that ruleth, with diligence; he that sheweth mercy, with cheerfulness. Distributing to the necessity of saints; given to hospitality. - Romans 12: 8, 13

   Therefore if thine enemy hunger, feed him; if he thirst, give him drink: for in so doing thou shalt heap coals of fire on his head. - Romans 12: 20

But to do good and to communicate forget not: for with such sacrifices God is well pleased. - Hebrews 13: 16

Use the things that God has given you (your possessions) to help others. And be happy when you do it! If you know someone that is hungry or thirsty, be the one to offer them help. God likes this kind of stuff.

Whoso stoppeth his ears at the cry of the poor, he also shall cry himself, but shall not be heard. - Proverbs 21: 13

By not doing so could affect your prayers.

4. We sacrifice with our love
   Let love be without dissimulation. Abhor that which is evil; cleave to that which is good. Be kindly affectioned one to another with brotherly love; in honour preferring one another; Not slothful in business; fervent in spirit; serving the Lord; Rejoicing in hope; patient in tribulation; continuing instant in prayer; Distributing to the necessity of saints; given to hospitality. Bless them which persecute you: bless, and curse not. Rejoice with them that do rejoice, and weep with them that weep. Be of the same mind one toward another. Mind not high things, but condescend to men of low estate. Be not wise in your own conceits. Recompense to no man evil for evil. Provide things honest in the sight of all men. If it be possible, as much as lieth in you, live peaceably with all men. Dearly beloved, avenge not yourselves, but rather give place unto wrath: for it is written, Vengeance is mine; I will repay, saith the Lord. Therefore if thine enemy hunger, feed him; if he thirst, give him drink: for in so doing thou shalt heap coals of fire on his head. Be not overcome of evil, but overcome evil with good. - Romans 12: 9-21

   This could be simplified by saying, "Be a good person." This is what God expects from us. He has already given the instructions in the Bible. All we have to do is read it and do what it says.

All of these are personal sacrifices that we can all make to God. We should give Him our best.

People That Forsake God
Thus saith the Lord unto this people, Thus have they loved to wander, they have not refrained their feet, therefore the Lord doth not accept them; he will now remember their iniquity, and visit their sins. Then said the Lord unto me, Pray not for this people for their good. When they fast, I will not hear their cry; and when they offer burnt offering and an oblation, I will not accept them: but I will consume them by the sword, and by the famine, and by the pestilence. - Jeremiah 14: 10-12

People get saved and they begin living their new life for God. All of a sudden, something deters them and they wander from their faith. They leave God behind. You're probably thinking, "There is no way that this could happen!" Unfortunately, it does.

There's many reasons why God's people have chosen to step away from Him. It usually begins my neglecting what they have learned from the Bible and putting a stop on their communications with Him by not praying. This makes them spiritually weak and they can easily fall to temptations and sin. As soon as sin enters their life, it begins rotting them to the core and eventually leads to death. If, by chance, they decide to pray for something, God won't hear them. They have forsaken Him.

The solution is to stay true to God always. Stay prayed up and in His Word. Allow it to strengthen you so that you can face temptations and turn away.

People Who Are Violent

And when ye spread forth your hands, I will hide mine eyes from you: yea, when ye make many prayers, I will not hear: your hands are full of blood. - Isaiah 1: 15

Who are the violent people of today? Many of them are the headlines of any media news outlet. There are also those that go unnoticed or unreported. Acts of violence happens every day - all over the world. It's sad, but it does exist. It will only get worse the closer it is to when Jesus returns.

Violence is defined as the intentional use of physical force or power, threatened or actual, against oneself, another person, or against a group or community, that either results in or has a high likelihood of resulting in injury, death, psychological harm, maldevelopment, or deprivation. For the record, I totally didn't write this definition of the word 'violence', but it contains enough details to give you an idea of what it means.

Violent people may pray, but unfortunately, God doesn't hear them.

People Who Worship Idols
Therefore thus saith the Lord, Behold, I will bring evil upon them, which they shall not be able to escape; and though they shall cry unto me, I will not hearken unto them. Then shall the cities of Judah and inhabitants of Jerusalem go, and cry unto the gods unto whom they offer incense: but they shall not save them at all in the time of their trouble. For according to the number of thy cities were thy gods, O Judah; and according to the number of the streets of Jerusalem have ye set up altars to that shameful thing, even altars to burn incense unto Baal. Therefore pray not thou for this people, neither lift up a cry or prayer for them: for I will not hear them in the time that they cry unto me for their trouble. - Jeremiah 11: 11-14

God doesn't like for His people to worship idols. The Old Testament contains stories of people that decided to go against God's wishes and do it anyway. There are also stories in there that tell of the consequences for disobeying God. They aren't pretty.

When it comes to praying, it seems that God doesn't hear the prayers of people that think it's cool to worship idols. I personally can't think of anyone today that melts gold and forms it into a statue, such as a cow, for worshiping purposes. But, that's how it was done in the old days. But, what about today? What are some modern day idols that we could be worshiping?

For us to recognize idols, keep in mind that we don't always have to use our eyes when it comes to dealing with spiritual idols. Idolatry is defined as anything... ANYTHING... that greatly consumes our thoughts, actions or resources or takes our focus off of God.

What are these things in our lives? Only you can answer for yourself, but there are numerous idols out there to choose from. If you were to make a list of all of the important things in your life, would it give you a clue?

Here are a few of those things that compete for our attention in today's world. These could become idols in our busy lives if we give them too much focus:

1. **People.** Many people in our lives can take the front seat, consuming our thoughts, actions and energy. This could be a spouse, a potential spouse, a boss or a child. This could be a celebrity or a public figure. In some cases this could even be a pastor or a church leader.
2. **Our Church.** The traditional church model is being replaced with the new modern church model. These new churches are offering programs, fancier buildings and better locations that has improved the way people go to church. Even though these features are awesome, these

things shouldn't prevent us from being disciples and reaching out to those that don't know Jesus.

3. **Our Ministry.** Believe it or not, ministry and religion are some of the easiest things in life to become idols. When you're involved in ministry at any level, it can be very easy to fall into a place of how much 'good' you're doing. We all need encouragement in ministry, but trying to receive it shouldn't be our focus. We have to keep a guard up against seeking out approval for what God decides to do through us or our work.

4. **Lifestyle and the Idol of Self.** Focusing our time, energy and money on our own personal wants and desires could become an idol. Trying to keep up with 'the Jones's' can be a bad thing and leave many of us in debt. This ever-growing debt can break up many good marriages and destroy lives. If you have ever bought something and gave the reason, "... because I deserve it.", this could be a potential sign of self idol worship.

5. **Our Challenges.** If there is one thing that can always take a person's eyes off of God, that would be life's challenges. Focusing too much on those challenges can rob them of any real accomplishments that God would bring into their lives.

6. **Social Media.** Here's another potential idol or idol of self in the form of likes, shares and follower counts. Billions of people are current users and we all are guilty of spending too much time on them. It has led to lower self esteem, depression and even suicide. Instead of signing off the social networks forever, it's now more important to be noticed in a stream of posts that more than 80% of our 'followers' will never even see.

We should probably set priorities in our life and make the choice to choose God as number one. Our focus should always be on Him. If we are guilty of putting Him at the bottom of the list or forgetting about Him at all, this could hinder our prayers.

People That Have No Faith
But let him ask in faith, nothing wavering. For he that wavereth is like a wave of the sea driven with the wind and tossed. For let not that man think that he shall receive any thing of the Lord. - James 1: 6-7

When we pray to God and ask Him for anything, we should have the faith in believing that God is able and can deliver. God wants us to trust Him and be confident when we pray to Him. The mindset should be like when we ask our earthly Dads for things. Hopefully, you grew up in a normal family setting where both parents were present. Unfortunately, it is rare.

Having faith in God when we pray would be knowing that we have a Heavenly Father that loves us and is there to help us in our time of need. As we live our life for God, He will help us build our faith in Him. He will answer prayers in a way that our confidence and trust in Him can grow. Every time that we pray, we need to always remember how He has helped us in the past. We should use this experience to continue building our faith. If we forget all that He has done for this, it will cause our faith to waiver. A faith that waivers will hinder our prayers.

People Who Mistreat God's People
Thou hast also given me the necks of mine enemies; that I might destroy them that hate me. They cried, but there was none to save them: even unto the LORD, but he answered them not. - Psalm 18: 40-41

Who hate the good, and love the evil; who pluck off their skin from off them, and their flesh from off their bones; Who also eat the flesh of my people, and flay their skin from off them; and they break their bones, and chop them in pieces, as for the pot, and as flesh within the caldron. Then shall they cry unto the Lord, but he will not hear them: he will even hide his face from them at that time, as they have behaved themselves ill in their doings. - Micah 3: 2-4

For a perfect world, people should love one another. If we all loved each other, there would be no need for wars. There wouldn't be any crime reported in the news. The downfall would be that many of our law enforcement folks would be out of a job.

The reality is that there is no perfect world. Actually, it seems like it's getting worse every day. The missing element in society is love. Many people have rejected God and, according to the Bible, God is love.

People can be mean and mistreat others. If you watch the news, you can see it every day. It's called crime and, according to the Internet, there are six types:

Violent Crime
murder, assault, kidnapping, manslaughter and rape

Property Crime
arson (to an extent), vandalism, burglary, theft and shoplifting

Public Order Crime
public drunkenness, prostitution, disorderly conduct, drug crimes and other alcohol-related crimes

White Collar Crime
fraud, bribery, identity theft, embezzlement and forgery

Organized Crime
gangs, the mafia and terrorists

High Tech Crime
fraud, illicit computer use, blackmail and hacking

According to the scriptures, unless these criminals get forgiveness for the wrong they have done to God's people, God won't hear their prayers.

When God Says No

When God Says No

There will be times when a person prays and they wont receive the expected result they were hoping for. Instead, God says, "No." They may decide not to accept His answer and say, "God didn't hear my prayer. He doesn't care about me." But, that isn't the case. God loves all of us and does care about us. He has reasons for why He says 'no'. Here are a few of them:

We have sin in our lives.
God is holy and sin is basically a wall between us and God. When we pray with sin in our lives, the prayer bounces off that wall. We need to confess our sins to God and ask for forgiveness.

If I regard iniquity in my heart, the Lord will not hear me: - Psalm 66: 18

Disobedience to God will keep that wall standing tall like a skyscraper and will always be a barrier for your prayers. It is best to make things right.

By saying 'yes' would bring harm that we didn't see coming.
God knows our past, present and future. He is always looking out for our best interest. When it comes to answering our prayers, a 'no' could turn out to be a blessing instead.

The thought that comes to my mind is in relationships. It's good to seek God in prayer when looking for your soulmate – your life partner. We may have someone in mind that we think would make the perfect match for us, but only God knows for sure. Praying about it is good. If the relationship hasn't manifested, it could be that God is protecting you from a future failure.

Here's another example.
Praying for a particular job or job position could result in a 'no', even if it seems like the perfect thing you need in your life right now. It pays more money, has great benefits and it could improve your lifestyle. But, if God says 'no', He may see something in that job that you aren't seeing. It could mean longer hours away from family. It could involve more stress which isn't good for your health. The answer for your money problem could be by simply getting rid of bills that you don't need.

We should always trust God when His answer is 'no'.

God has something far better for us.
We pray for something that we think is exactly what we need in our life, but it never happens. God says 'no', If it's a true need, God knows about it and will supply our needs. It could be that the 'particular item' that we are asking for isn't what He has in mind.

I hate car problems. Having to repair a car myself is stressful. I know that I don't have enough skills to be a mechanic. When you're broke and have a car problem, you become the only mechanic that you can afford.

There was a time when our only running vehicle decided to stop running properly. As a non-mechanic with no abilities to diagnose the problem, I was placed in a very stressful position. I had to fix this car. The bad thing about this situation was that it happened during a time when our bank account was starving to death. What could I do? Thankfully, I knew God was there to run to when problems popped up in my life. So, I prayed about it.

"Dear Lord, my car is broke and so am I. Please send me a new one because I need it." At this point of my life, a new car would be a 'need'. Without a car, you can't buy groceries. You can't go to work to make money to support your family. There's no other way. A new car is what I needed – or so I thought.

As I waited for this new car to miraculously fall from the sky or pull up in my driveway, I kept the faith that God would answer my prayer. Days passed and still no new car. Instead, I was hitching rides to get to the places I had to go. Finally, as a last resort, I had to humble myself and borrow a vehicle from my Stepdad. He is a good person and would have loaned it to me on day one, but there's something about being a grown man and having to borrow from your parents. I don't like doing it.

During the borrowing process, my Stepdad learned that I had a car that was broken down. Because he is a car enthusiast, he had the connections to get my car hauled to a mechanic that worked from home and was knowledgeable and affordable to get the job done. I was able to continue life with a borrowed car until mine was fixed.

But, why didn't God just say 'yes' to my prayer request? A new car would have been a perfect gift. It's probably because He knew that I couldn't afford the car payments and insurance at the time. Maybe God knew that I needed to humble myself and remove the pride of asking for help when I desperately needed it. Maybe my Stepdad needed a blessing from God for helping me and my family. It could be that the mechanic needed to hear about Jesus or maybe he had been praying for financial help. There's no telling how much spiritual stuff that was going on with this situation. But, God saw the bigger picture and knew what we all needed in our life.

Having a running vehicle that was paid for was the better option for me at the time.

We pray for the same thing as another believer.

Let's say two Christians are praying for the same job. God will have to answer 'yes' to one and 'no' to the other. Who He decides to get the job is up to Him, but I'm sure that He will have something good for the other person, too.

I can't think of any situations in my life where this has happened to me, but I'm sure it happens in other people's lives. Just know that God doesn't love one person more than the other, but He does know what is best for us.

The Lord will perfect that which concerneth me - Psalm 138: 8

I like this verse because it tells me that God has a perfect plan for me. Regardless of how God decides to answer our prayers, it will be perfect according to His plan. We simply have to trust Him and His decision.

We pray for things where a 'yes' is impossible.
God can do anything. He has proven time and time again that He can work miracles in my life and in the lives of others.

But Jesus beheld them, and said unto them, With men this is impossible; but with God all things are possible. - Matthew 19: 26

For with God nothing shall be impossible. - Luke 1: 37

When it comes to prayers, some things should not be asked of God. And it's not that He couldn't answer the prayer with a 'yes', I think some things should be considered 'impossible' and left alone. Here's a few examples:

Praying for a loved one to return from the dead is just not going to happen. I'm not saying that God couldn't do it, because He did it in the Bible... in the story of Lazarus. I just feel that everyone has an appointed time to leave this world and we shouldn't expect to change it.

A new baby is born into the world and it's a girl. The parents were hoping for a boy and feel like it's not too late. They know God can do the impossible and decide to pray for Him to turn their baby girl into a boy with fully functional moving parts and everything. I'm pretty sure God will say 'no'.

An elderly woman is tired of being old. The aches and pains, the wrinkles and droopy skin parts have become too depressing to bear. The lady decides to pray to God to make her young again. She wants the body and looks she had when she was 20. Personally, I think she is asking a little too much. I would almost guarantee God would say 'no' to this one.

Yes, God can do the impossible. I just think some things should be left alone.

God didn't say 'no' – He said 'wait'
We get discouraged when we feel God has said 'no', but the fact is that He really didn't say anything at all. Believe it or not, 'wait' is an answer. God uses delays to answering prayer to build patience, persistence and build our faith. There's a lot that goes on during the waiting period. We will discuss this further in the next chapter.

For now, just remember waiting is important.

God's 'no' isn't rejection – it's redirection
Delight thyself also in the Lord; and he shall give thee the desires of thine heart. - Psalm 37: 4

God knows the desires of our hearts. Even when we pray, He already knows what we are going to ask Him for. He is our Father in Heaven and wants what is best for us. It's similar to our earthly father... or better yet... if you are a father, you know what it's like when your kids need something from you. You will try to give it to them. Right? Sometimes we give it to them even if Mom doesn't want them to have it, right? That's just what Dads do. But, we do know when to draw the line.

And I say unto you, Ask, and it shall be given you; seek, and ye shall find; knock, and it shall be opened unto you. For every one that asketh receiveth; and he that seeketh findeth; and to him that knocketh it shall be opened. If a son shall ask bread of any of you that is a father, will he give him a stone? or if he ask a fish, will he for a fish give him a serpent? Or if he shall ask an egg, will he offer him a scorpion? - Luke 11: 9-12

But, also as their father, you want what is best for them. Sometimes that means telling them 'no' for something that you know isn't good for them. Instead, you give them what they actually need.

"Dad, I'm hungry."

"What do you feel like eating?"

"Well, I'm craving chocolate cake with sprinkles."

"Definitely not! It's 8:00 am and you haven't even had breakfast yet. How about a sausage egg biscuit with hash browns?"

"Uggh! I guess that will do..."

For some of us Dads, we may think deeper into this whole chocolate cake thing and realize it's made from milk and eggs – which is considered a breakfast food – and may give in to their need. However, we may remove the sprinkles.

God may decide to answer our prayer request with a 'no' and give us something that is much better. I know I use my example of 'how God fixed my car instead of giving me a new one' a lot when I share how God has answered my prayers. But, it's a cool example of how God thinks and how He knows what's best for me. Basically, I needed a car during a time when the economy sank. No funds means no car – it was an impossibility. So, I prayed – I prayed big.

"Lord, send me a new car."

He basically told me 'no' to my prayer – even though I thought it was a need – and He chose to get my existing vehicle fixed instead. He supplied my need, but He went further than that. He knew I didn't need a car payment and that paying for full coverage insurance on a new vehicle would have been hard for my family to manage. And if you think about it, my old car became somewhat new again when it got fixed.

Answered Prayers
Why Did I Have To Wait So Long?

Answered Prayers – Why Did I Have To Wait So Long?

It's good to know that, if we ever have a need in our life, we can always ask God for it in prayer. He may or may not answer the prayer request right away, but He will answer. It's always in His timing – not ours. I have learned this lesson so many times in my life.

For people like me, we want to be in control of the things that go on around us. We try and plan our steps. We know the things we need to help us get from Point A to Point B. We have already wrote it down in a notebook – we've planned it and broke it down into easy steps. As a Christian, we have God to supply those needs. In our minds, He becomes more like a 'storehouse' - a supplier of needs – that we use to help us on our journey that we've planned through life. As long as our steps move smoothly, we won't call out to God as much. But, if we reach a stumbling block or if things don't go the way we have planned, we call out to God in prayer. To continue our journey, God must act fast in His reply. I mean, we have already planned everything out and all that God has to do is supply the need. Right? We've even did the hard part by figuring out the 'specific need'. He doesn't have to spend unnecessary time trying to figure anything out – all He has to do is deliver – with no delay. Life is busy and we're on an important mission – *chop chop!*

This mentality towards God sounds funny, but many of us are guilty of treating Him this way. We simply don't want to wait. But, because He loves us, He allows us to wait to teach us important life lessons. It's interesting to know, that while we are waiting, our brains will go into hyper-drive with all kinds of spiritual thoughts about Him and ourselves.

Does God hear me? Is He even listening?
And this is the confidence that we have in him, that, if we ask any thing according to his will, he heareth us. - 1 John 5: 14

The first thing I do when I pray is to ask God for forgiveness of any sin in my life. The reason I do this is that the scriptures say that He won't hear us if any exists. I figure what's the point of praying a whole bunch of words if He won't listen until the sin issue has been resolved. That's why I take care of that first. I call it 'opening up the communication lines'. If you have prayed for something and feel that God isn't listening, it could be that He wants you to get that sin out of your life. Ask Him to forgive you.

According to 1 John 5: 14, as children of God, we can be confident that God will hear our prayers. The world isn't so big that He doesn't have time for us. We are equally important to Him. I used to wonder why He would take the time to hear my prayer, especially when there are millions of other people around the world praying, too. Why should He be focused on my problems? I am just a speck of sand in a very large sandbox. The key here is that He loves us. It's something that may be hard for us to wrap our minds around.

While we are waiting for our prayer to be answered, we can use this time to comprehend this love He has for us and become confident in knowing that He will hear us when we pray.

Does God care? Does He really love me?
If ye then, being evil, know how to give good gifts unto your children: how much more shall your heavenly Father give the Holy Spirit to them that ask him? - Luke 11: 13

For I am persuaded, that neither death, nor life, nor angels, nor principalities, nor powers, nor things present, nor things to come, Nor height, nor depth, nor any other creature, shall be able to separate us from the love of God, which is in Christ Jesus our Lord. - Romans 8: 38-39

The Lord is good to those who wait for him, to the soul who seeks him. - Lamentations 3:25

The scriptures tell us that God loves us. It's easier to 'read' than it is to 'accept' personally. But, if we were to look around us and see all that God has done for us, it should give us a sampling of His love. The air that we breathe, the water we drink and the food we eat could be considered as 'love basics'. It's always been provided by Him, but we tend to take it for granted.

Then as we look at the things we have personally, such as a home – a place to sleep and shelter us - God's love becomes a little more personal. Can you imagine what it would be like to be homeless? Isn't it nice to have a place to sleep? We have these things because God has provided them to us. That's God's love.

If we were to look a little deeper than that, we would see that we have our family and friends – we're not alone. We have jobs and an income which provides for our needs and wants. The feeling of His love is getting stronger.

If we took another step closer, we could see the fine details that God performed when He created us. Everyone is basically the same, but each of us has something that makes us unique.

Everyone is different and that's by God's design. That's personal love.

During this waiting time, you might want to learn how much God truly loves you.

Do I really need God? Should I try to answer my prayer on my own and supply the need myself?
Trust in the Lord with all your heart, and do not lean on your own understanding. In all your ways acknowledge him, and he will make straight your paths. - Proverbs 3: 5-6

But as for me, I will look to the Lord; I will wait for the God of my salvation; my God will hear me. - Micah 7:7

I believe that I shall look upon the goodness of the Lord in the land of the living! Wait for the Lord; be strong, and let your heart take courage; wait for the Lord! - Psalms 27: 13-14

If you read the Bible, you will discover many stories of people that trusted God and depended upon Him for their needs. Even in situations where it seemed like they knew the correct answers, they would seek and follow God's guidance instead. And many times they would have to wait until they heard from God first.

Moses was a man called by God to do an important task. There was no way he could free God's people from Egypt in his own strength and abilities. Sure, he could've tried, but probably would have died in the process. There are several people like this in the Bible whose story is an example of how we need God and should wait for His answers. Read about Noah, Abraham, Daniel, and Joseph. That's a just a few off the top of my head. Each one had their own personal experience with God. Their experience strengthened their faith and they became 'faith' examples to others.

Some people want results and they want them now. When it comes to prayer answers, you are almost guaranteed to have to wait. This waiting period will test your true faith in God.

Do you really trust Him to answer? You may have deep rooted issues with trusting people. Somewhere down the line someone has let you down and now you have a hard time with trust. And now you have a hard time trusting God with your prayers. It could be why you are having to wait. God is building your trust in Him. Wait for Him.

God hears the prayers of His children? Oh wait!... did I lose my salvation again?!!

And I give unto them eternal life; and they shall never perish, neither shall any man pluck them out of my hand. My Father, which gave them me, is greater than all; and no man is able to pluck them out of my Father's hand. - John 10: 28, 29

According to the scriptures, our salvation is secure. Waiting for an answer to a prayer for a lengthy period of time could create some doubts in our mind. The sad thing is that 'being secure in our faith in Jesus' is the foundation for Christianity. Doubting it every time there is a delay in answers to our prayers is what the Bible calls 'a wavering faith'.

Let us hold fast the profession of our faith without wavering; (for he is faithful that promised;) - Hebrews 10: 23

But let him ask in faith, nothing wavering. For he that wavereth is like a wave of the sea driven with the wind and tossed. For let not that man think that he shall receive any thing of the Lord. A double minded man is unstable in all his ways. - James 1: 6-8

During this waiting period, root yourself firmly in knowing that your faith in Jesus is secure. Never doubt it again.

Waiting Produces A Character That Is Pleasing To God
Be still before the Lord and wait patiently for him; - Psalms 37: 7 a

Rejoice in hope, be patient in tribulation, be constant in prayer. - Romans 12: 12

but they who wait for the Lord shall renew their strength; they shall mount up with wings like eagles; they shall run and not be weary; they shall walk and not faint. - Isaiah 40: 31

God wants His people to trust and love Him. He also wants them to know that He is worthy of our trust and that He loves us. If we are waiting for a prayer to be answered, it could be that He is working on the other side of that prayer and putting things together for us. Or, He could simply want us to learn a very valuable spiritual lesson during our waiting time.

As Christians, we are followers of Christ. From the day we became saved, God began a work in us to become more like Jesus. We will go through life experiences that will build our character. Yes, it would be nice if we all went to Jesus School and learned everything in a classroom setting – by doing our homework and taking tests. But, that's not how it works. Everything is learned through life experiences. God uses our daily journey in life – the good and bad things that happen – to mold us. Waiting for a prayer to be answered is part of it.

Like I said earlier, there's so much stuff that bounces around in our minds when we are waiting. We question God and we question ourselves. We look for weaknesses in our spiritual life and we question God's role in our life. But that's OK. It's part of the molding process. It builds our character.

What exactly are the characteristics of Jesus that God wants us to have? Here are 10 of them:

- Compassionate
- Servant attitude
- Loving
- Forgiving
- Committed
- Prayerful
- Gentleness
- Patience
- Self-Control
- Humble

These are the characteristics of Jesus. These are the same ones that God wants to develop in us. Allow Him to work in you and mold you to become the person He wants you to be.

Remembering What We've Prayed

Remembering What We've Prayed

Remembering What We've Prayed

Wherefore remember, that ye being in time past Gentiles in the flesh, who are called Uncircumcision by that which is called the Circumcision in the flesh made by hands; That at that time ye were without Christ, being aliens from the commonwealth of Israel, and strangers from the covenants of promise, having no hope, and without God in the world: But now in Christ Jesus ye who sometimes were far off are made nigh by the blood of Christ. - Ephesians 2: 11-13

This scripture is part of a letter written by Paul to the Ephesians. They were Gentiles that, according to the law, weren't allowed to be part of God's big happy family. They weren't Jews. But, because of what Jesus did on the cross, they now had an opportunity to become adopted. Paul wanted them to remember where they came from – lost without hope. By remembering, they could strengthen their faith and find joy regardless of their current situation.

This rule could apply to our prayers. Every time we face a situation, and we decide to pray to God about it, we should remember it. We should also remember how God answered the prayer. Our memories will help us to reflect on how awesome

God is in our life. It will remind us of how He is able to work miracles, so that any time we face an obstacle, we will remember that God will help us through it when we pray to Him. Remembering will strengthen our faith, make us more confident and bring joy to our life regardless of what is currently happening around us.

For some of us, remembering things can be difficult. I don't think I have the mental capacity to hold a lot of memories. That's why I narrow those thoughts down to what I consider important. My wedding anniversary, the birthdays of family members and my kid's names are some of the things I try to remember. Every now and then I will forget and I will have to ask my wife to remind me. But, that's OK. I'm old and that's to be expected.

How could we remember our prayers? Even the most miraculous answer from God to one of our prayers could one day be forgotten. What could we do to keep that memory alive?

I use a notebook for everything. I make lists for things I need to do around the house. I have learned, that if I write it down and keep this notebook on the table beside my recliner, I will see it enough every day that it will force me to get those listed items done. It sounds weird, but it works for me. I think my wife likes my notebook idea because she doesn't mind contributing to it, too.

We could do the same with our prayers. Start listing them. Write down what we are praying for and leave enough space for how God answers it. It will also help us in being persistent in prayer because, if God hasn't answered it yet, that would mean to continue praying about it. Over time, we will have a notebook full of our prayers that we can reflect upon. We could also share them with our family and friends to give them encouragement in their similar situation. The notebook could also become our testimony to them of how God helped us.

Another good way to remember answered prayers is to turn them into decorative wall reminders. Some folks might write them on post-it notes and stick them everywhere in their house, but that could look weird. Plus, if you stick them in a room that has a ceiling fan, it could be noisy or it could cause them post-it notes to fly all over the place. It's probably not a good idea. But, there are other ways to decorate our walls with prayer reminders.

Moses and Aaron from the Old Testament were instructed by God to keep things and place them in an ark to remind them of their experience with Him.

"...the ark of the covenant overlaid round about with gold, wherein was the golden pot that had manna, and Aaron's rod that budded, and the tables of the covenant..." - Hebrews 9: 4b

They kept a golden pot of manna (the breakfast food that God supplied every morning on their journey), Aaron's budded rod and the tablets that contained the Ten Commandments in an ark that was placed in the tabernacle so that everyone could see it. This was their reminder of all that God had done for them when He set them free from Egypt.

Keeping a visible reminder of what God has done in our lives isn't something new. Undoubtedly, God thought it was a good idea. He told Moses and Aaron to do it. Maybe we could incorporate this idea into our lives, too.

If you have a camera, you could take pictures of God's answers to your prayers. As a photographer, your photo becomes a work of art that can be framed and hung on a wall. This may sound crazy, but let's say your refrigerator stopped working and you didn't have the funds to buy a new one. You prayed about it and God supplied the need. Well, take a picture of that refrigerator and place it in a decorative frame. Hang it up in the kitchen. And the next time you have company over for dinner and they ask, "Why do you have a picture of a refrigerator hanging on your wall?" You can say, "It's a reminder of how God got me one when I didn't have a way of getting one for myself." It is now a testimony of faith and it gives glory to God.

Let's say you had a bill that you couldn't pay last month. You prayed about it and God supplied your need. That 'paid in full' receipt or bill becomes a reminder that would look pretty cool placed in a picture frame on a fireplace mantle. You agree?

Use your imagination on how you could display the things that God has done for you. Just remember that the purpose is to create memories to reflect upon and share with others.

Sinner's Prayer? What Is That?

Sinner's Prayer? What Is That?

The Internet tells us that the Sinner's Prayer (also called the Consecration Prayer and Salvation Prayer) is an evangelical Christian term referring to any prayer of repentance, prayed by individuals who feel convicted of the presence of sin in their lives and have the desire to form or renew a personal relationship with God through Jesus Christ.

In my opinion, it is the most important prayer a person can pray. This prayer, if done with the right motives and with sincerity, determines our life's existence after the current one fades away.

To get a better understanding of why a sinner's prayer is important, let's take a quick look at the whole picture. God, the Creator of everything, is holy. And we, as part of His creation, are separated from Him because of sin. Sin is the bad 'stuff' that we do that goes against His way of life. To bridge the gap between us, God sent Jesus to die as a sacrifice for sin. Jesus is the bridge that allows us to be reconnected with God. All we have to do is sincerely repent of our sins and believe in Him. You're probably wondering, "What's this got to do with me?"

Well, if you've never made the choice to make Jesus your Lord and Savior and asked for forgiveness of your sins, then you are separated from God. This is a serious situation. It's a choice of eternal death or eternal life for you.

Jesus – The Bridge To God
God loves us. This includes everybody. If you are walking and breathing in this world today, He loves you. However, sin separates us from Him because He is holy. He sent us a Savior – Jesus, His Son – to rescue us from sin so that we could reconnect with Him. All we have to do is believe in Him.

For God so loved the world, that he gave his only begotten Son, that whosoever believeth in him should not perish, but have everlasting life. - John 3: 16

Salvation (being saved from sin) isn't something we have to earn or work towards. It's a free gift given by the grace of God. We become saved by having faith in Jesus.

For by grace are ye saved through faith; and that not of yourselves: it is the gift of God: - Ephesians 2: 8

If we choose to believe in Jesus, we become sons of God. We become part of God's family.

But as many as received him, to them gave he power to become the sons of God, even to them that believe on his name: - John 1: 12

There is only one way to God and that is through Jesus. Some people believe they have to work for it or do good deeds. No. It's only through faith in Jesus.

Jesus saith unto him, I am the way, the truth, and the life: no man cometh unto the Father, but by me. - John 14: 6

Jesus is the only way for salvation. There's not a human being on the face of the Earth that can save you – only through Jesus.

Neither is there salvation in any other: for there is none other name under heaven given among men, whereby we must be saved. - Acts 4: 12

Forgiveness of sins can only be done through Jesus. He paid that price with His death on the cross.
And he is the propitiation for our sins: and not for ours only, but also for the sins of the whole world. - 1 John 2: 2

For he hath made him to be sin for us, who knew no sin; that we might be made the righteousness of God in him. - 2 Corinthians 5: 21

Sin
Sin is any thing that goes against God's way of life for us. Everyone sins. We are all going to do something sinful. It's just part of our DNA.

For all have sinned, and come short of the glory of God; - Romans 3: 23

As it is written, There is none righteous, no, not one: There is none that understandeth, there is none that seeketh after God. They are all gone out of the way, they are together become unprofitable; there is none that doeth good, no, not one. Their throat is an open sepulchre; with their tongues they have used deceit; the poison of asps is under their lips: Whose mouth is full of cursing and bitterness: Their feet are swift to shed blood: Destruction and misery are in their ways: And the way of peace have they not known: There is no fear of God before their eyes. - Romans 3: 10-18

You Have A Choice: Eternal Death Or Eternal Life
We have a choice. Sin leads to death, but we can choose to have faith in Jesus and receive eternal life.

For the wages of sin is death; but the gift of God is eternal life through Jesus Christ our Lord. - Romans 6: 23

The Remedy
Because of God's love for us, He sent Jesus to die as a sacrifice for the sins of the world.

But God commendeth his love toward us, in that, while we were yet sinners, Christ died for us. - Romans 5: 8

The only step we have to make is to call out to Jesus and accept Him as our Lord and Savior. We have to believe that God raised Him from the dead. We should turn from our sinful lifestyle and begin following Him.

That if thou shalt confess with thy mouth the Lord Jesus, and shalt believe in thine heart that God hath raised him from the dead, thou shalt be saved. - Romans 10:9

For whosoever shall call upon the name of the Lord shall be saved. - Romans 10: 13

Therefore being justified by faith, we have peace with God through our Lord Jesus Christ: - Romans 5: 1

God's Promise – A Relationship Of Peace
A life lived for Jesus is a changed life that offers peace. We are eternally secure knowing that we are now part of God's family.

There is therefore now no condemnation to them which are in Christ Jesus, who walk not after the flesh, but after the Spirit. - Romans 8: 1

For I am persuaded, that neither death, nor life, nor angels, nor principalities, nor powers, nor things present, nor things to come, Nor height, nor depth, nor any other creature, shall be able to separate us from the love of God, which is in Christ Jesus our Lord. - Romans 8: 38-39

Now It's Your Turn
No where in the Bible does it say that repeating a prayer saves anyone. However, it does involve calling out to Jesus. I believe a Sinner's Prayer is a good way to call out to Him. I do need to stress the fact that **repeating prayers will not save you**. Salvation begins by recognizing that you are lost in sin and that you need forgiveness. You also believe in the death and resurrection of Jesus Christ. You want a changed life and you want to live your life for Him. This is the heart you should have when you want to be saved.

Where do you stand today? Do you need Jesus in your life?

This is a sample of a Sinner's Prayer for you to use. As long as you feel convicted in your heart and are sincere about wanting this change in your life, repeating this prayer will help:

"Dear Lord Jesus, I know that I am a sinner and I ask for Your forgiveness. I believe You died for my sins and rose from the dead. I turn from my sins and invite You to come into my heart and life. I want to trust and follow You as my Lord and Savior."

My prayer for you is that you will always live your life for Jesus. Allow Him to work in you and through you to mold you into the person He wants you to be. Your life won't always be easy but it will be peaceful.

Where do you stand today? Do you need Jesus in your life?

This is a sample of a sinner's prayer for you to use. As long as you feel convicted in your heart and are sincere about wanting this change in your life, repeating this prayer will help:

"Dear Lord Jesus, I know that I am a sinner and I ask for Your forgiveness. I believe You died for my sin and rose from the dead. I trust and follow You and invite You in. I do my best, but like, I want to start and follow a new Lord and Savior."

My prayer for you is that you will always live your life for Jesus. Allow Him to work in you and through you to mold you into the person He wants you to be. Your life won't always be easy but it will be peaceful.

122

What Does It Mean to Be A

Christian

Written and illustrated by Jeff Todd

Introduction

The guidelines for Christian living have already been written. You can find everything you need to know right there in God's Holy Word - The Bible. It's just a matter of opening it up and reading it. The Spirit of God will reveal to you the things you need to know and give you the ability to understand them.

The purpose of this book is not to be a substitute for reading the Bible. Oh no! Everyone should read it. My hope and intentions for writing this book is that it will inspire you, as the reader, and will offer humorous illustrations to use in your walk with Christ and to put Christianity out there in an easy to understand format. Together we can learn to live our life to the fullest with happiness and joy that God intended for us to live.

First of all, being a Christian doesn't have to be boring and dull. I believe it should be energetic and alive. We are to be a light in the world that we live in and shine out to others. When a person sees the way we are, it should make them want to be that way, too

Our lifestyle should point them to Jesus. Everything we say and do should reflect the One that saved us.

I have never considered myself to be like everyone else. The way I look at life may be different than the way others see it. Even as a young child, Christian people to me were always the suit and tie-wearing folks or the snooty ladies wearing the dresses and they acted very *'stiff necked'*. It was almost like they were afraid to smile.

I agree, it was wrong of me to segregate Christians like this, but those were the Christians I knew. As I grew older, I realized that not all Christians were like this and were actually normal people.

Being called into the ministry, I have to use what the Lord has given me. This includes the relationship I have with Jesus through His grace that saved me, His Word, and the gifts, talents, and characteristics that He gave me.

When you put that all together in a mixing bowl, you have:

ARTISTIC
FUNNY
SAVED
MINISTER

I know from experience that being a Christian isn't a difficult task. It's not a series of rituals or following a magic formula. It's actually so simple that anyone could do it.

That's my purpose and focus of writing this book! I want to write something that would minister to people (no matter who they were) and possibly help them understand what being a Christian is all about. It's got to be simple and easy to understand. I don't use BIG words when I speak, so why should I write BIG words when I am using this to reach people and lead them to Jesus. I can't! It's not how God made me!

If you're reading this today, this book is for you from a simple minded person like me. Being a Christian is awesome and it's not as weird as you may have heard. We're not crazy people! If you have never asked Jesus to come into your life, I hope and pray that you make that choice today.

If you're already a Christian, I hope this book ministers to you, too. Living the life you profess isn't as hard as you make it when you realize what it's all about. Actually it's not supposed to be hard at all. You're a Christian because you gave your life to Him. Sometimes we have to give it back to Him and let Him lead the way.

Excuse me for a moment. I'll be right back. I need to pray!

Dear Lord, I pray right now that You use these words from this book to reach people out there. I don't know who this is intended for or who will be reading this. I know that I belong to You and that You will use me for your glory. Please do so today. Thank you Jesus. Amen.

So, here it is folks!

What Does It Mean To Be A

Christian

The Starting Point: Jesus

Christian living begins with having Jesus Christ in your life. Period.

Let me say that again because it's important.

Christian living begins with having Jesus Christ in your life. This means that before you can live the life of a Christian, you have to have Jesus as your Lord and Savior in your life. He has to be the center of your life; the foundation that your life sits on. You can't live a Christian life if you're not a Christian.

No *'buts'* about it!

But, I Go To Church

Going to church does not make you a Christian. It makes you a *'church-goer'*. Even though you attend church every Sunday, in the morning and at night, it doesn't make you a Christian. You may be a Sunday school teacher and teach from the Bible. It doesn't make you a Christian.

It's almost like calling yourself

a fisherman without a fishing pole. Yes, you may go to the lake, but without a pole, you're just a...person that goes to the lake. You may know everything there is to know about fishing. You may know the different types of fish by the color of their fins and the number of sparkles in their eyes, but it doesn't make you a fisherman. You may have the best fishing boat on the lake, but without the pole, you are basically a boat owner. Are you with me?

But, I Have Christian Family

Just because one of your family members is a Christian doesn't make you one. I know this will be hard for people to believe, but being a Christian is not a genetic thing. It's a Jesus thing!

"My grandfather was a deacon at Flakey Biscuit Baptist Church. He was a Christian man that loved the Lord."

That's great! But, it doesn't make you one. The glitter from your Christian relative's walk doesn't magically fall off on you. It would be nice if it did, but it doesn't. Being a Christian and being saved is about a one on one relationship with Jesus Christ.

But, I Shook The Preacher's Hand Last Sunday

If *'hand shaking'* guaranteed a Christian life, then everybody that visited a church on a Sunday morning would be saved and so would every person that the preacher had come in contact with outside of the church. Think about it! Hand shaking is a greeting, not a magic salvation ticket! That's not how it works!

The Deal?

Here's the deal! A person can only become a Christian when they accept Jesus into their life and get saved. Saved? That's right! The day you realize that you are a sinner and that you are lost without a Savior is the day you have a choice of whether to be a Christian or not. The sad thing is that we are all sinners!

For all have sinned, and come short of the glory of God - Romans 3:23

It's like a day at the lake. You jump in and realize you can't swim! Life was pretty smooth when you were playing close to the bank. But as you drifted out towards the deep part of the water, you realize that you needed a float. The same is true in life. You need to be saved or you will sink like a rock!

"That sounds all fine and dandy, but what am I being saved from?"

The answer is sin. It's those *'bad things'* in your life that goes against God and His way of life. To realize how bad sin is, you must first know who God is.

Who Is God?

God created everything. There is nothing in this world, on Earth, or in outer space that He did not create. He created the water, the air, the trees, animals, and He even created you.

The Bible tells us that He knew us before we were even born and that He knew ALL about us. That tells me He's the one that put us here. He put you here!

Before I formed thee in the belly I knew thee; and before thou camest forth out of the womb I sanctified thee, and I ordained thee a prophet unto the nations. – Jeremiah 1: 5

I believe that we are all here for a purpose - His purpose. But, we will never know this purpose until we give our lives to Him. For a God that created everything in this universe to take the time to make me, tells me I have a purpose for being here. The same is true for you! We need to find out what it is. This will involve getting to know the Creator.

Have you heard this one

before?:

For whom he did foreknow, he also did predestinate to be conformed to the image of his Son, that he might be the firstborn among many brethren. – Romans 8: 29

He wants a relationship with you. Since you are here and have a purpose, you will need to get a relationship started with God. You will need to know more about Him. The Bible says God is holy and perfect - sinless. Now keep that thought in your mind for a moment and let's talk again about sin.

When you think of the sin in the world today, what comes to mind? Does murder and stealing? What about lying and foul language? There are all kinds of sin! Small ones to big ones and they all have one thing in common - they are still *'sin'*. Sin is what separates us from a relationship with God. We live in a sinful world and we have sin in our lives. How can we make things right? The unfortunate thing is that WE can't! We need something or someone to fill in that gap. God knew this, too. So what needs to happen? Don't worry! God already had that planned out because He loves us.

Here's what God did for us! He sent His only Son to die as a sacrifice for our sins. It sounds like a drastic measure to take but it's what was needed. Jesus, His Son, died for us so that we could live - eternally with God.

But wait! His death required something from us?

That's right! It says we have to BELIEVE in Him. Here's another scripture you may have heard:

That if thou shalt confess with thy mouth the Lord Jesus, and shalt believe in thine heart that God hath raised him from the dead, thou shalt be saved. - Romans 10:9

FOR GOD SO LOVED THE WORLD, THAT HE GAVE HIS ONLY BEGOTTEN SON, THAT WHOSOEVER BELIEVETH IN HIM SHOULD NOT PERISH, BUT HAVE EVERLASTING LIFE. - JOHN 3:16

It sounds to me like God has provided a way out for us, but He also requires us to do something to be saved. We already know we are a bunch of sinners. Right?

We are to confess with our mouth the Lord Jesus? And believe in our heart?

Sounds too simple to be true, doesn't it?

It is and it starts with a simple prayer to God. After that, all we have to do is receive this gift of salvation. I believe God convicts our hearts that we are lost. It's like a helpless feeling you have inside that let's you know that you need Him in your life.

Are you feeling that right now? If so, let's get this thing settled. I know a lot of religious people and some Christians get 'weirded out' when you present a model prayer to the lost and ask them to repeat it. I can understand their way of thinking and I know that just repeating prayers doesn't save a person. It has to be heartfelt and sincere. The main points of your prayer has to cover knowing that you're lost without Jesus in your life, understanding that you're a sinner that's sorry for the junk you're doing, and that you are willing to turn from that junk and want Jesus to come in and take over.

That's basically it!

So, if you meet that criteria and would like to accept Jesus as your Lord and Savior, let's do this thing together.

SINNER'S PRAYER
(A SIMPLE EXAMPLE)

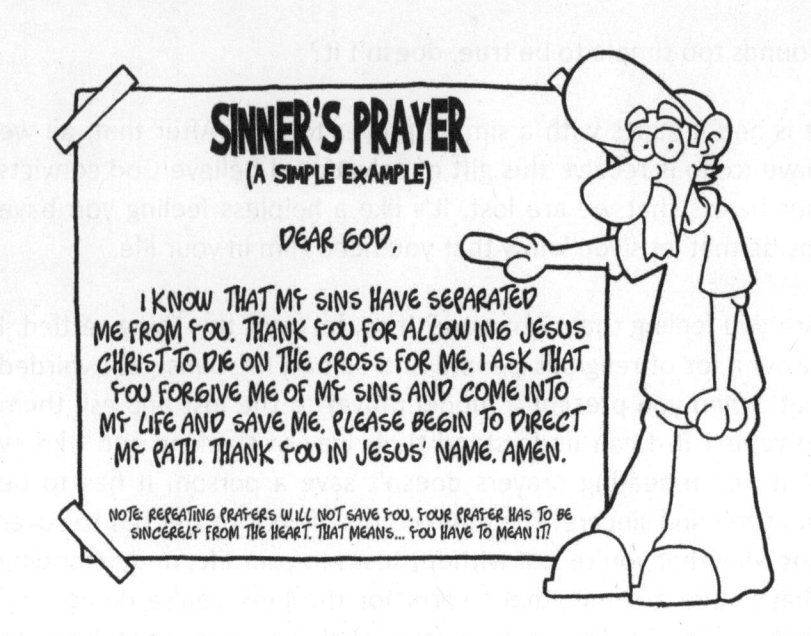

DEAR GOD,

I KNOW THAT MY SINS HAVE SEPARATED ME FROM YOU. THANK YOU FOR ALLOWING JESUS CHRIST TO DIE ON THE CROSS FOR ME. I ASK THAT YOU FORGIVE ME OF MY SINS AND COME INTO MY LIFE AND SAVE ME. PLEASE BEGIN TO DIRECT MY PATH. THANK YOU IN JESUS' NAME. AMEN.

NOTE: REPEATING PRAYERS WILL NOT SAVE YOU. YOUR PRAYER HAS TO BE SINCERELY FROM THE HEART. THAT MEANS... YOU HAVE TO MEAN IT!?

That was easy, wasn't it? Now, I know sparks aren't flying around you and choirs of angels aren't floating by with harps. But, inside you will feel a sense of relief.

It will feel like a ton of bricks have been lifted off your shoulders. Your life may not even show changes immediately, but from this point forward it will. It's like being a new little plant. You will begin growing. That's why they call it being 'born again'. You have a new life! It's up to you make it grow. You can do this by going to church, reading the Bible, and praying every day. Every step in your life from this day on is a *'stepping stone'* towards Jesus and growth in your spirituality.

Spiritual Fertilizer

"I'm saved and I know where I'm going when I die. I'm cool with that! But, what should I be doing until then?"

The answer is simple! I should be growing! You should be growing, too! The day we got saved started a new life in us. This is very similar to growing turnip greens in a garden. This new life started as a small seed planted in the ground. Even as a small seed, it's still a turnip green! But you know as well as I do that a plate full of seeds doesn't taste the same as a big plate of turnip greens. The seeds need to grow first.

To help a turnip green grow, it needs some food. Right? It needs some good soil, refreshing water, and some sunlight. The same is true in our Christian walk. Yes, we could stay content with being a seed. But, wouldn't it be better if we started sprouting? A Christian needs some spiritual fertilizer - some food for the soul.

God provides us with ways to grow. All we have to do is use what He gives us. The soil He provides us is through the relationship we can have in Him through prayer and walking with Him daily. Every day is an opportunity.

We just need to take advantage of it.

Finding a Bible-believing church and actually going to it is a great starting point for growth. I will be the first to admit that going to church was not in my plans. As a young saved *'whooper-snapper'*, I wasn't really a *'people'* person and I hated getting up early on a Sunday morning to hear a long-winded preacher spitting and slobbering on the whole congregation.

The music in church was awful and would always come from people that really shouldn't have been up front singing to people anyway. I spent my time in the back row socializing with my friends. I was young and didn't know what the whole *'church thing'* was about and what it was for.

Church: The Growth Experience

Now that I am older, I realize that it was for my spiritual growth as a baby Christian.

This process of getting up on a Sunday morning, getting dressed, and going to a building and hanging out with all of these *'weird'* people was intended to help me grow. My job was to listen and learn.

I also realize that my attitude towards it was wrong and sitting on the back row was my first mistake. For a young teenager like me, I should have been on the front row listening. Now that I look back, maybe my life wouldn't have drifted away from God as it did. I'll explain more on this later on in this book.

What is *'going to church'* all about?

A church building is a place where believers gather to worship and praise God. It's just a building and as I explained earlier, by *'just going'* doesn't save you. Only God can do that! We go there to worship Him and praise

Him for who He is – He's God!

It's also a place to *'get your learning on'*. This is accomplished by singing praises, praying, and listening to what the preacher has to say. God uses these tools to teach us stuff from His Word.

> *O come, let us sing unto the LORD: let us make a joyful noise to the rock of our salvation. – Psalm 95: 1*

Depending on the church, the music is a big part of worship. There are many scriptures throughout the Bible that encourages us to sing songs of praises to God. Actually, the Book of Psalms is simply a book full of song lyrics. It can be in a traditional music style or contemporary music style. It really doesn't matter as long as it's joyful. People will argue about the type of music being played at church and say that only one style is acceptable, but it's not about the style as it is the *'heart'* in which it's worshiped. No one ever taught me this concept about Christian music, but it was in the Bible if I had just taken the time to read it. Plus, when you are singing with right heart, the bad singers start to sound pretty good. Our focus is more on what they are singing instead of how well they sing it. And that's the truth!

A preacher plays a big part in the service because he is a God-called man to deliver the Word. He is the guy that stands in the front of the church with the suit on. If you are in a Baptist church, you will recognize him because he will be the one that speaks the loudest and has the biggest belly. He will be the sweaty man that spits on the congregation sitting on the front row during the services. He is also the first one in line at the *'all you can eat'* buffet dinner restaurant after the church services are over. I'm sorry. I had to throw that in there.

Being a preacher is a big responsibility. The Lord gives him a message to share with the people at church. It is up to him to deliver it. If he delivers something that was not given to him by God, he is going to be in some serious trouble. The preacher has to be very careful in his preaching. He is responsible for what comes out of his mouth.

Preachers ain't perfect! They're human just like we are!

On the flip side of this, we have to realize that the preacher is just a man. He will make mistakes and is not perfect. Many people will stop going to a particular church or to church, in general, because of something a preacher did that was not acceptable. We should not be followers of preachers, but followers of Jesus Christ. However, we should listen as the Word is being presented to us and follow along with our Bibles open. Listening was another mistake I made earlier in my life.

Prayer: For More Growth

Praying is our way of communicating with God. Just like with all types of relationships, good communication is the way to make it stronger. That's why a lot of marriages don't work out. Many times it's because one person does all the talking, or no one is listening, or that nobody talks or listens at all. It just doesn't work!

Prayer keeps our spiritual life alive! Don't you want to live? Get your prayer on!

By praying to God, we can ask for forgiveness of our sins. We can tell Him how our day is going and let Him know the areas we need help. We can ask for things in our life and even pray for other people's needs. It's like talking to a good friend or better yet, we are talking directly to our Father in Heaven. It helps us to grow spiritually, especially when we see the things we pray for come to pass.

Praying is done in church. It can be done as a group or you can pray as an individual at the altar or right where you sit. But, it's not the only place! You can pray anytime and anywhere. You can pray at home, at somebody else's home, or even on aisle 3 at your local Wally World. It doesn't matter as long as you pray! Most importantly, pray daily!

Bible: The Growth Continues

There's a book that sits around in many homes all over the world. It's usually the one that's tucked away with dust covering it. It's called the Bible. Even though many people own it, it's rare that people actually read it! For a Christian, it's like an instruction manual for living. It's food for the soul. Its God's words in book form so that we can grow spiritually.

The problem is that many people see it is as just a book with words; like a hard to read novel. It's full of *'thee's'* and *'thou's'* and it's hard to understand. It has stories in there that really don't apply to us, right? Wrong!

Living the Christian life requires reading the instruction manual.

Have you ever tried to put something together or use something without the manual? There were always parts left over or it didn't work the way it's supposed to. Right?

The same is true in our Christian walk. If you try it without the manual, you'll end up face down in the middle of the road. I know from experience, but I am thankful that Jesus was there to pick me up!

There is so much stuff written in the pages of the Bible. It covers everything! Any topic you want to know about, it's in there! There's anything from basic life principles to the history of man. It does include stories of people and their experiences. Why? The purpose is so that we can use their life of accomplishments or mistakes to help make ours better. We can learn from them. It's so cool! The more you put into it, the more you will get out of it.

To sum it all up, basic spiritual growth begins with going to church, prayer and reading the Bible. You can only grow from here!

The Battle Is On! Like A Chicken Bone

Just when you thought that being a Christian was easy, bad things come into your life. Troubles seem to come at you like darts flying at you from everywhere. It may seem like you are now being tempted with things from your past. You may be tempted with things that affect your weaknesses. It's all part of the plan.

It's a battle and we have an enemy! Satan is his name. You may have heard of him. Don't be '*skeered*'! He's not that cute little cartoon you see on television and he's not that scary demon you see in the horror movies. According to the Bible, he is an angel – a fallen angel. He was with God before the world began. He has been trying to mess things up from the day that God created Adam and Eve.

Remember hearing about Adam and Eve?

In the first few chapters of Genesis, you'll read where Satan tempted them into eating the forbidden fruit. By doing so, sin began and it has been growing ever since. He is in the world today along with his band of devils trying to trip people up. He tries to prevent people from getting saved and makes life hard for the average Christian. The purpose in all of this is to mess up God's work in this world and in His work in the people that live in it.

Keep this in mind, God is creating and preparing a place for His people. Folks, this world that we currently live in is not our home! He is returning one day to take his people to their real home. Who gets to go? It's the people that have been saved. That is why Satan works so hard. His days are numbered and he already knows where he's going and it's not good. His purpose is to take people with him - the lost and unsaved. Did you get that?

I bet you're thinking...

I'm saved, so why is he messing with me?

That's an easy question to answer. You could be the link to someone else getting saved. Your witness and testimony could be what leads them to a relationship with the Lord. You will notice that he works on you the hardest when you are trying to live right. If you are living sinfully, Satan doesn't have to do much to you. You have already lost your witnessing ability. What else does he need to do? He's got you right where he wants you - **DEFEATED**.

But, as you grow in the Lord, you are gaining strength and will be used to reach others. Satan hates this idea and will start throwing the darts. He wants you dead and out of the picture! You have become a hindrance to his master minded plans. Watch out!

That's why it is so important to apply the *'spiritual fertilizer'* to your life - church, prayer, and Bible. When you are following Jesus, you will be able to recognize Satan's devilish schemes against you.

There hath no temptation taken you but such as is common to man: but God is faithful, who will not suffer you to be tempted above that ye are able; but will with the temptation also make a way to escape, that ye may be able to bear it. – 1 Corinthians 10: 13

Here's where it gets tricky. As a child of God, He is watching over you. There is nothing that Satan does to you that God doesn't know about. As mean as it may sound, God allows Satan to tempt you. Yep! That's right! We can learn this from the Book of Job. This doesn't make God bad! It is part of His way of strengthening you as a Christian.

However, He will never let you be tempted more than you can bear without His help!

Temptations are coming. What are they? These will be the things that come into your life that make you think,

"Hmm...Should I or shouldn't I?"

This could be almost anything. Temptations come from Satan and are directed by God. As we discussed earlier, temptations will either make us stronger or they will defeat us if we agree to give in to them.

You can almost know what your temptations will be by knowing what your weaknesses are. If the Lord rescued you from abusing drugs and alcohol, you can be guaranteed that these will come back into your life in the form of a temptation. The temptation in itself is not wrong, it's when you give into them that it becomes a sin. Are you hearing me?

Many people suffer from spiritual depression because they don't know why they are being tempted with these things that may have destroyed them in the past. They think it's their fault and feel like they have been defeated. Here's your wake up call! It's just a temptation! That's all! Rebuke it and send it back to Satan from where it came! Keep moving on and get over it! Don't let it get you down! If you're down and out because of it, then Satan has won the battle anyway.

Once again, temptations come from Satan. Always remember that! It's important to know.

> ***Submit yourselves therefore to God. Resist the devil, and he will flee from you. – James 4: 7***

Trials, on the other hand, are a different story. What are trials? I'll try to explain. Trials, sometimes called *'valleys'*, enter our lives from time to time. They usually appear when things seem to be going great.

They can almost be like a messed up deer hunting trip. You deer hunters will be able to relate to this. You are wearing your camouflage sitting up in a deer stand. Everything is going great! You have your gun ready and deer are everywhere! It's going to be a great hunting day! All of a sudden it starts to rain! The deer scatter and you have to climb down from the tree soaking wet. Your legs start chaffing as you walk the long trail back to our 4 x 4 pick up truck. You are feeling miserable and you weren't able to get a deer.

Why did this have to happen? Why do you have to go through this?

You call your friend, Bob, on your outdated cell phone telling him what you just went through as you drive back home disgusted with the way the day ended. You are going through all kinds of emotions. You are mad, sad and everything else other than glad. You know what I'm saying?

The next day, you try hunting again. Before you leave, you check the weather report on the news to see if it will rain. The weatherman says, *"It will be sunny all day!"* You bring an umbrella and an extra pair of socks anyway – just in case. This time you pull your trailer carrying your ATV (All Terrain Vehicle) that you got for Christmas last year with you in case of an emergency. Now you are prepared and learned a lesson!

The purpose of this long drawn out story is to say that God is ultimately in control and allows trials to happen in your life to make you stronger. There is something about them that help you develop character. They make you better prepared for future trials and you are able to use the experience to teach others and help them. Remember Bob from the story? Guess what? He doesn't go deer hunting anymore without bringing an extra pair of socks because he learned something from your experience, too. Pretty cool, huh?

Just like temptations, trials seem to focus on your weak areas in your walk with Jesus.

Suppose you have a love for money and material things. Guess what your trial will be? Yep, you guessed it! Money issues! It could happen in the form of losing your job or down time in your business. Who knows? But, the important things you will learn from it are to trust God with all of your heart, He is your provider – NOT YOU, and to be content with what you have. I know this one from personal experience.

What if you have anger issues? Guess what your trial will be? You will be hit with things in order to make you mad. You will eventually learn to control your temper and thank God for working with you.

The victories come when we *'pass the tests'*. When you are tempted and you are able to push it away, you have just won a victory. Congratulations!

When you are in a trial and you make it through praising God, you have just won a victory. You are on a roll! Now take a look at yourself. You are stronger, better, and more usable to God to win others to Him. It's all part of the process and you're in it! Why would God go through all of this trouble for you?

That's an easy one. He loves you!

The final victory comes when Jesus returns to take us home to be with Him. What an awesome day that will be! Now that you know the basics of being a Christian and what it's all about, it's time to *'walk the walk'*. This means *'being a light in the world'* and sharing what you know about Jesus. I would be lying to you if I said it was easy. It's not! The temptations and the fact that we are all just too lazy prevent us from doing everything the Lord requires us to do.

Walkin' the Walk

There are a lot of people out there that will say that they are a Christian. It's not up to us to decide if they are speaking the truth. This is up to them and their relationship with God. But, I believe if we are going to say we are a Christian, we need to show it in the way we live our lives. We need to 'walk the walk'.

As a child of God, our life should show a change. That means we shouldn't be doing the old sinful things we used to do. This life should reflect Jesus. Have you heard the old saying, "What would Jesus do?"? This question could be applied to every choice we have to make.

I also know that we aren't perfect. We are going to make

mistakes. But, we shouldn't let that way of thinking prevent us from trying. We should strive to be like Jesus every day.

Here's an example:

What if the tire company, **Not Good Enough Year**, thought the same way. What if they thought, "Well, I know I'm supposed to make good tires and that people out there depend on me to provide them, but I'm not perfect. So, I'll just sit here and sorta throw something together and see what happens."

I imagine a lot of people driving cars and trucks will be affected by it. Some will end up in ditches and may never get to their destination. You see where I'm going with this? It's about making the effort to do the best you can. People's lives are at stake!

'Off' With The Old And 'On' With The New

Before you were saved, you may have been in a lifestyle that you know Jesus wouldn't approve of. This could be almost anything. I won't sit here and list the many things that could fall in this category because you know the ones that pertain to you. These made up the 'old' self of your sinful nature.

Now, here's the problem. You are saved and still doing the *'old'* things that you used to do. Your *'new'* life doesn't reflect a change. You are not living by what you read in the Bible or what you are being taught at church, but by your sinful nature. It could be that you are not reading the Bible or going to church at all and are just *'winging'* your new Christian walk. It's not going to work!

This creates a bad situation in your relationship with Jesus and to others around you. You are missing out on the spiritual joy of being saved. You are basically the 'old' you with a Jesus label. This is good if all you want is a free ticket to Eternity. But that's not what being a Christian is about. God has a purpose for you and will use you, if you let Him, to reach out to others. That's when *'being saved'* gets exciting and has a greater meaning in your life. Allow Him to change you!

The Suit And Tie Christian

Before I start on this topic, let me tell you that wearing a suit and tie is not a bad thing. Actually, Christians that wear suits and ties look good and I mean that. That is the main purpose of saying it: Christians that just *'look'* good. A person could be sinfully rotten to the core, but when they put a suit and tie on, they fit in with the rest of the Christians in church on Sunday morning.

Being a Christian is a spiritual thing - it's what's on the inside that counts. It's a relationship with Jesus Christ that goes straight to the heart. When this kind of relationship goes to the heart, it will begin to manifest itself outwards in our actions and in our words. Are you with me?

Many people are deceived by the *'suit and tie'* Christian because they only *'look'* good. If you were to spend some time with them, you would realize what is really going on in their heart. You could see it in their actions in the way they conduct their life. When they speak, their words coming out would make you think differently of them.

Knowing that, it is important to realize that *'walking the walk'* is more than just trying to look good. It's about *'looking good'* because of the relationship we have in Jesus and what He has placed in our heart.

Holier Than Thou Christian

I have met some Christian people that are quick to judge people. Being a Christian myself, these people were quick to tell me everything that I was doing wrong. This made me want to quit going to church and socializing with the 'Christian' people. I later learned that this type of judging is OK when you are trying to help someone and are doing it in a loving way. This should also be followed by a solution to their problem.

Pride is a killer, folks! People can easily fill themselves with the pride of being a Christian and the spiritual things they know that not only do they kill their witnessing abilities but they actually kill the chances of bringing others to Jesus. They can also kill the growth of other Christians. It's a bad deal! Jesus wasn't about all that!

If you read the Bible and learn how Jesus was, you'll learn that He never had this type of attitude toward others. He had compassion for His followers in teaching them how they should and shouldn't be and He had compassion for the ones that didn't know Him. By His example is why people chose to follow Him. He would socialize with the sinners and lead them by being the example. He didn't walk around with a stick bopping people on the hands every time they did something wrong. If He did see something wrong in a person's life, He would lovingly tell them and provide a solution. This is how we should be.

It's great to be a Christian and to have grown spiritually in our walk. But we need to understand that without God's mercy on our life and His spiritual guidance, we are nothing more than a sinner ourselves. When we meet people that are lost, we need to focus on the sin in their lives and not on that person.

And remember God loves them, too.

It's Not Just About Us
It's About Others

The day we became saved, God could have just taken us home to be with Him. We're saved! What other reason would we need to be here on Earth? Since we don't belong here anymore, we may as well just move on to Glory Land. So, why are we still here?

Listen to this:

Go ye therefore, and teach all nations, baptizing them in the name of the Father, and of the Son, and of the Holy Ghost: Teaching them to observe all things whatsoever I have commanded you: and, lo, I am with you alway, even unto the end of the world. Amen. – Matthew 28: 19, 20

Jesus said it right there. We are called to be His disciples to go out and teach others. A disciple is a follower of Jesus; to follow His teachings and to be like Him. Just like the twelve disciples in

the Bible, we have a mission statement:
"To be a light in the world and to lead others to Jesus by spreading the Gospel and being an example to the world."

Being a Christian means being Christ-like. You may not know this, but being a Christian is not just about you. The world teaches us to be concerned about ourselves and nobody else. What do we want out of life? How can we make our life better? Watch television and you will discover that all of the commercial ads are directed to you.

This is not what Jesus is all about. Your Christian life should reflect the One that saved you. Why is this so important?

Here's the scenario:

- **The world is full of people that don't know Jesus as their Lord and Savior.**
- **Jesus is returning one day to take His children home.**
- **The ones that remain will burn in a lake of fire.**

Who are His children? It's the people that are saved. Does He want everyone to spend Eternity with Him? Yes, He does. Unfortunately, it's this thing called 'sin' that we talked about a few pages back that separates us. He gives us all a *'freedom of choice'*. It's a choice to turn from sin, ask for forgiveness and to turn to Him. It's plain and simple! We have a choice!

What is our role as a Christian in all of this? The answer is to lead others to Him. It's about *'being a light in the world'*. We are the link that connects them to a relationship with Jesus. We can't save them, but we can lead them to the One that can. Is this sinking in?

This is why it's so important to truly *'walk the walk'*. It's not so that WE can live a better life, but to show others the *'better life'* we have in Jesus. Think about it!

When you start living the life Jesus wants you to have, people are going to want it, too. If they don't see a change in you, then how will they know Jesus? Time is running short! What are you waiting on? Walk the walk! Be a light!

My Testimony

A testimony is what you have after the Lord saves you or delivers you from something. It's like our story to tell others of what Jesus has done for us. Every Christian will have one. If you are saved today, you have one, too.

Our testimony is what we will use to lead others to Jesus. It is how we are able to witness to other people. Believe it or not, that *'thing'* that Jesus delivered you from is probably what is holding a lot of people you meet back from a relationship with Jesus. It is very interesting how this works. It's like God will put people that are not saved in your life that will need to hear your testimony. The amazing thing is that they are going through the same thing or have been through it and don't know how to deal with it. All of a sudden they meet you; a person with a similar story, but this time there is a solution. His name is Jesus.

I accepted Jesus as my Lord and Savior when I was 14 years old. My father had left me and my mother when I was five and she was forced to raise me on her own. The Lord stepped in during my teenage years because I needed a father in my life. He became my Heavenly Father!

Do you realize what happens to many teenagers growing up without a father? Let's just say that many of them end up going down the wrong roads in life. They wind up in places and situations that they shouldn't be in. God gave me His protection and put me on the path of righteousness as long as I stayed focused in it.

Within that same year, I also met Satan. I didn't really recognize him at first because he disguised himself in the things I allowed in my life. Pornography was his first trick. This is a big temptation for a young kid with raging hormones, but I took the bait. This went on for years and found its way on my computer screen as I got older.

Satan also knew I had a passion for music. I enjoyed listening to it and playing it on the guitar. Its original purpose was intended to glorify and praise God, but wound up on the stages at the local bars playing as a live band.

This introduced a new temptation given by Satan that created an addiction within me that I would later battle with in life. It's the poison called alcohol. It destroys you from the inside out and affects the people around you. Alcohol every day pushes the family away! And that's exactly what it was doing. Because of my addiction, I would be re-creating my life story all over again with my kids. They would be fatherless and the vicious cycle would continue.

That's when Jesus showed up! He woke me up when my son got saved. At that time, my son needed someone to lead him to the Lord and I wasn't able to do it. I should have been, but couldn't. My life was a mess! I had to take him to someone that could. This burned me deep and helped me realize that I needed Jesus back in my life, too. It wasn't that I need to be saved again. It was that I needed to go back to where I left Him. I had turned away.

Years later, the pornography is gone and the alcohol has been traded in for the living water that Jesus freely offers. I have been *'living'* since then. This new change has created a great life for me and my family. It has created a ministry that God has used has to reach many people and touch lives. I realize now that this was part of God's original plan before I decided to change it. I am ashamed that it took twenty years to wake me up. This is my testimony. Thank you Jesus!

Once again, the main purpose of this book is to use what the Lord has given me to share with you.

My heart goes out to all Christians everywhere – all over the world. If the lessons I have learned from my life can be used to help someone out there, then that's what I want to do. I'm sure there are Christian people out there like me that don't know what the whole deal is. Some are blinded by Satan on their purpose on this Earth and what they should be doing until the Lord comes back. I hope this book will prevent them from wasting 20 years of their life going in the wrong direction.

If you don't know Jesus as your Lord and Savior, I encourage you to make that step. Being a Christian isn't what the world says it is. It's being what Jesus wants us to be: happy and full of joy. If you need that in your life today, Jesus can and will freely give it to you. All you have to do is ask Him.

If you're a Christian, begin living by His Word and reading it daily. Don't sit around like stagnated water! Do something with the new life God has given you. Reach out to people that need this life, too. Learn more about Jesus. Live the life that He wants you to live. It brings life – life abundantly. Let's do something! You know?

I hope you received what you needed today. And please share this book with someone you know!

More From A BackPew Review

Thanks for reading this guide. We hope you enjoyed it and will continue to read our other guides in the series. Here is a complete list of our books from the series:

- What Does It Mean To Be A Christian
- Acts: The Early Days Of The Christian Church
- Being A Dad According To The Bible
- The Prison Letters: Apostle Paul's Letters To The Early Church
- Exodus: The Journey To The Promised Land
- Genesis: The Beginning, The Fall And The Promise
- The Seven Letters: The New Testament Letters To The Early Church
- The Gospel From A Four-Sided View
- Healthy Eating: A Few Tips From The Bible
- Being A Man According To The Bible
- A Marriage Built To Last: Learn What The Bible Says About Marriage
- How Do I Pray? The Bible Tells Us How
- Revelation: The End Is Near?

Milton Keynes UK
Ingram Content Group UK Ltd.
UKHW040358291024
450367UK00011B/155